COOKBOOK
FOR
MEN

FROM MEAT AND SEAFOOD TO JERKY AND WILD GAME, FROM SMOKING AND GRILLING TO CAST IRON CAMPING

ROGER MURPHY

CONTENTS

INTRODUCTION

"THE ART OF MAKING MEAT, SEAFOOD, AND WILD GAME " CATCHES THE SPIRIT OF IRRESISTIBLE DISHES FROM AROUND THE WORLD, BRINGING TOGETHER VARIOUS RECIPE LISTINGS, FROM SUCCULENT BEEF AND JUICY PORK TO LOVELY SALMON AND TENDER SHRIMP.

DIVE INTO THE CULINARY DEPTHS WITH THE COMPREHENSIVE GUIDE FOR MEN THAT SHARES VALUABLE TIPS ON SOURCING THE RIGHT INGREDIENTS AND PROVIDING COOKING TECHNIQUES LIKE SMOKING, GRILLING, CAMPING, AND MUCH MORE TO ENSURE FLAVOR AND EXCELLENCE WITH EVERY MEAL. WITH STUNNING PHOTOGRAPHY AND EASY INSTRUCTIONS, THIS COOKBOOK IS YOUR TRUSTED COMPANION IN YOUR QUEST FOR SUPERIOR VEGGIES AND DESSERTS.

TIPS

FOR SMOKERS

- When you are ready to cook, preheat your smoker to 225°F (110°C) for 12-15 minutes
- Use wood chips that are recommended for this recipe
- When the smoker has reached the desired temperature, put an additional batch of wood chips in the wood chip tray
- Fill the water pan with the cider brine and to the level recommended in the smoker manual and replenish as necessary

FOR GRILLS

- Always refer to your grill's manual for specific preheat times and instructions.
- For CHARCOAL grills, remove any ashes and preheat for 20 minutes. Open the bottom vents to allow maximum airflow. Start the grill using a small amount of lighter fluid and a chimney starter or old newspaper. You will find the correct charcoal size and shape for your specific model in your appliance's manual.
- For GAS grills, preheat for 10 minutes. While lighting, ensure the lid is raised. Turn your propane tank's valve to open. Turn on one burner press the grill's ignition button. When the first burner is lit, continue to turn on as many burners as needed. Make regular checks of the grease trap. You will also need to brush the grill regularly to prevent debris from piling up.
- For WOOD PELLET grills, fill the hopper with your choice of pellets. Plug the appliance in, and flip the power switch to the ON position, with the lid open. Set the dial to SMOKE for 5-7 minutes. When you hear the wood pellets entering the fire pot and grill is beginning to produce white billowing smoke, select your chosen temperature on the dial. Next, close the lid, and depending on your desired temperature, preheat for approximately 10 minutes. Check your aluminum foil-covered drip pan is in place and that the grease bucket is in position. Brush the grill grates if necessary and place in position. When the grill is at the desired temperature, you can begin grilling.

FOR CAMPING

- How to prepare your campfire for cooking: Get the fire started using your choice of fire starter. Once the kindling begins to break down, add large pieces of split, dry, seasoned wood, alternately around the fire in a teepee shape. Leave room for air to reach under the wood, and take care not to smother the fire.
- Continue to add more wood until there are 6-8 logs engulfed entirely in flames.
- Maintain the fire, keeping the heat while avoiding large open flames. Doing this will help you achieve an even cook.
- Always have a bucket of water close by for stray embers or in care the fire gets out of hand

MEAT CUTS

SMOKED BEEF RIBS

PART 1 MEATS

CHAPTER 1

BEEF

SMOKED BEEF RIBS

INGREDIENTS FOR 4 SERVINGS

THE MEAT

- 1 4-bone section beef ribs (4-lb, 1.8-kg)

THE INGREDIENTS

- Horseradish flavor Dijon mustard, any brand – 2 tablespoons
- Beef rub, any brand – 6 tablespoons

THE SPRITZ

- Hot sauce, any brand – ¼ cup
- White vinegar - 1 cup'

THE SMOKE

- Set the smoker to 250°F (120°C) for indirect cooking
- Hickory or oak wood chips work well for this recipe

METHOD

1. Cover the beef ribs with the flavored mustard, and season generously all over with beef rub.
2. Transfer the ribs to the preheated smoker, and insert a meat thermometer, programmed to 200°F (90°C) in the thickest part of the ribs while not touching the bone. Close the smoker's lid and smoke the ribs for 3 hours.
3. Add the hot sauce and white vinegar to a spray bottle and shake to combine.
4. Once the ribs have smoked for 3 hours, start to spritz them every 40-60 minutes. Continue to smoke until they register an internal temperature of 200°F (90°C). The whole smoking process will take approximately 8-10 hours.
5. Take the beef ribs out of the smoker and wrap them in aluminum foil. Set aside to rest in an insulated cooler for a minimum of 60 minutes before slicing.
6. Enjoy.

SMOKED BEEF BRISKET

INGREDIENTS FOR 6-8 SERVINGS

THE MEAT

- Beef brisket (3-lbs, 1.4-kgs)

THE RUB

- Worcestershire sauce – 3 tablespoons
- Coca-cola – 1 cup
- 3 garlic cloves, peeled and minced

THE SMOKE

- Preheat your smoker to 220°F (105°C)

METHOD

1. Add the brisket to a large ziplock bag. Pour the Worcestershire sauce, coca-cola, and garlic cloves to the bag and chill overnight.
2. The following day, take the beef out of the bag and place on the smoker. Cook for several hours or until the meat registers an internal temperature of 145°F (65°C) for medium-rare or 150°F (70°C) for medium.
3. Take the beef out of the smoker, cover loosely with foil and allow to rest for 10-15 minutes.
4. Slice against the grain before serving.

SMOKED TRI-TIP STEAK

INGREDIENTS FOR 8 SERVINGS

THE MEAT

- Tri-tip steak beef, patted dry (3-lbs, 1.4-kgs)

THE INGREDIENTS

- Kosher salt – 3 tablespoons
- Freshly ground black pepper – 3 tablespoons

THE SMOKE

- While the smoker is cold, add oak wood chips to the wood tray
- Set the smoker for indirect cooking to 225°F (110°C)

METHOD

1. Rub the meat all over with salt and pepper.
2. Smoke for 60-90 minutes until the meat registers an internal temperature of 130°F (55°C).
3. Remove the meat from the smoker and wrap tightly in parchment paper. Return the meat to the smoker and cook for an additional 30-60 minutes until it registers at an internal temperature of 140°F (60°C).
4. Remove the meat from the smoker and set aside for 20 minutes before slicing against the grain.
5. Serve and enjoy.

CHIMICHURRI STEAK SKEWERS

TOPIC: GRILLING   **TOTAL COOK TIME 35 MINUTES**

INGREDIENTS FOR 4 SERVINGS

THE MEAT

- Flank steak (1-lb, 0.5-kg)
- 8 wooden skewers

THE INGREDIENTS

- Salt – 1 teaspoon
- Ground cumin – ½ tablespoon
- Black pepper, to taste

THE CHIMICHURRI

- Extra virgin olive oil- ½ cup
- 2 garlic cloves, peeled
- Fresh cilantro, chopped – ¾ cup
- Red wine vinegar – 2 tablespoons
- Red pepper flakes – ½ teaspoon
- Fresh lemon juice – 2 tablespoons
- Salt – ½ teaspoon
- Black pepper, to taste

METHOD

1. Soak 4 wooden skewers in a bowl of water for 20 minutes.
2. Slice the flank steak into 16-20 strips.
3. Season the steak with salt, cumin, and black pepper to taste.
4. Thread the steak strips onto the prepared wooden skewers in accordion style. Set to one side for the moment.
5. Next, make the chimichurri. Add the olive oil, garlic, cilantro, red wine vinegar, red pepper flakes, lemon juice, salt, and black pepper to a food processor and blitz until well combined. Set to one side.
6. Lightly grease the grill grates with oil.
7. Place the steak skewers on the grill and cook to moderately high heat for 1 minute on each side until browned.
8. Take the skewers off the grill and brush with the prepared chimichurri.
9. Serve and enjoy.

BEEF AND SALSA BURGERS

TOPIC: GRILLING   **TOTAL COOK TIME 15 MINUTES**

INGREDIENTS FOR 4 SERVINGS

THE MEAT

- Minced beef (8-oz, 220-gm)

THE INGREDIENTS

- Wholemeal breadcrumbs (3-oz, 85-gm)
- 1 small onion, peeled and grated
- Carrot, grated (3-oz, 85-gm)
- Worcestershire sauce – 1 teaspoon
- Small handful fresh parsley, chopped
- Salt and black pepper to season
- 4 wholegrain buns
- Tomato ketchup – ¼ cup

METHOD

1. In a large bowl, combine the minced beef, breadcrumbs, onion, carrot, Worcestershire sauce, and parsley. Season with salt and black pepper.
2. Shape the mixture into four evenly-sized burger patties.
3. Cook the patties on the grill for 4 minutes on each side until evenly cooked. Take the patties off the grill and set aside in a warm container.
4. Toast the wholegrain buns on the grill for 30-60 seconds.
5. Arrange the burger patties in the toasted buns and top each with a spoonful of salsa.
6. Serve straight away.

SIMPLE BEEF CHILI

INGREDIENTS FOR 16 SERVINGS

THE MEAT

- 90 % lean ground beef (4-lbs, 1.8-kgs)

THE INGREDIENTS

- Canola oil – 2 tablespoons
- 2 medium-size onions, peeled and chopped
- 1 medium-size green pepper, chopped
- 4 cans kidney beans, rinsed and drained (15-ozs, 425-gms) each
- 6 cans stewed tomatoes, cut up (15-ozs, 430-gms) each
- 1 can beef broth (15-ozs, 430-gms)
- Chili powder – 3 tablespoons
- Ground coriander – 2 tablespoons
- Ground cumin – 2 tablespoons
- 4 cloves of garlic, peeled and minced
- Dried oregano – 1 teaspoon

METHOD

1. Start your campfire and set up a 12-ins (30-cms) deep Dutch oven for cooking.
2. In the Dutch oven, over moderate heat, heat the oil.
3. In batches, brown the beef, crumbling it with the back of a spoon as it cooks until no pink remains. Drain the fat and put it to one side.
4. Add the onions along with the green pepper to the Dutch oven and cook until fork-tender.
5. Return the meat to the Dutch oven and stir in the remaining ingredients (kidney beans, canned tomatoes, beef broth, chili powder, coriander, cumin, garlic, and oregano).
6. Bring the chili to boil before reducing the heat to a simmer, while covered, until the flavors are incorporated. This will take around 90 minutes.
7. Serve and enjoy.

STEAK WITH RED WINE SAUCE

STEAK WITH RED WINE SAUCE

TOTAL COOK TIME 20 MINUTES

INGREDIENTS FOR 4 SERVINGS

THE MEAT

- 2 sirloin steaks (12-oz, 340-gm) each

THE INGREDIENTS

- Olive oil – ½ tablespoon
- Salt and freshly ground black pepper to season
- 1 medium shallot, minced
- Red wine – 1 cup
- Beef broth – 1 cup
- Cold butter, chopped into small pieces – 2 tablespoons
- Parsley, chopped – 2 tablespoons

METHOD

1. In a large cast-iron skillet, heat the oil over moderately high heat.
2. Season the meat on both sides with salt and lots of black pepper.
3. Once the oil is smoking lightly, add the steaks to the pan.
4. While turning every 60 seconds for 8 minutes, cook the meat until the steaks are browned but don't yield to the touch.
5. Remove the steaks from the skillet and transfer to a chopping board, to rest.
6. Add the shallot to the skillet, and sauté until softened for 60 seconds.
7. Pour in the red wine and beef broth, scraping up any browned bits from the bottom of the pan.
8. Cook over high heat for 5 minutes until the liquid is reduced by around 75 percent.
9. Remove the skillet from the heat, and one piece at a time, whisk in the butter. Stir through the parsley.
10. Slice the steaks into thick pieces, and arrange them on 4 warmed dinner plates.
11. Pour the red wine sauce over the steak, and enjoy.

BEEF CURRY

TOTAL COOK TIME 1 HOUR

INGREDIENTS FOR 4 SERVINGS

THE INGREDIENTS

- Ground beef (1-lb, 0.5-kgs)
- 1 onion, peeled and diced
- 2 celery stalks, trimmed diced
- 1 large carrot, trimmed and chopped
- Garden peas, frozen – ½ cup
- Garlic powder – ½ teaspoon
- Ground ginger – ¼ teaspoon
- Medium heat curry powder – 1½ teaspoons
- Basmati rice, uncooked – 1½ cups
- Water – 3½ cups
- Salt – ¼ teaspoon

METHOD

1. Prepare your campfire for cooking.
2. You will need a 12-ins (30.5-cms) Dutch oven with 6 coals around it and 18 on its lid. The desired cooking temperature is 350°F (180°C).
3. Add the ground beef to the Dutch oven, and with a wooden spoon, break up the meat. Stir until browned all over.
4. Add the onion, celery, and carrot and while cook while stirring for 3 minutes.
5. Next, add the peas, garlic powder, ground ginger, and curry powder, stir well to combine for 2-3 minutes.
6. Stir in the basmati rice and pour in the water. Stir to combine and bring the mixture to a boil.
7. Taste the curry, and season with salt.
8. Place the lid on the Dutch oven and reduce the heat by moving it further away from the middle of the coals.
9. Allow the curry to simmer, stirring every 10-15 minutes, until the rice is cooked. The whole cooking process will take around 35-40 minutes.
10. Serve and enjoy.

HAWAIIN PULLED PORK

CHAPTER 2

PORK

HAWAIIN PULLED PORK

TOTAL COOK TIME 14 HOURS 20 MINUTES

INGREDIENTS FOR 18-20 SERVINGS

THE SEAFOOD

- 1 pork shoulder (6-lb, 2.7-kg)

THE CHEESE SAUCE

- Butter – 1 tablespoon
- Flour – 1 tablespoon
- Milk – ¾ cup
- BBQ rub – 1 tablespoon
- Cheese, shredded – 2 cups

THE INGREDIENTS

- Olive oil – 1 tablespoon
- Pork and poultry BBQ rub, any brand – 3 tablespoons
- Pineapple juice, divided (24-oz, 600-gm)

THE SMOKE

- Set the smoker to 225°F (130°C)
- Cherry wood pellets are a good choice for this recipe

METHOD

1. For the cheese sauce, melt the butter in a pan, add the flour and combine. Pour in the milk and mix well.
2. To the butter mixture, stir in the BBQ rub and incorporate.
3. Begin adding the cheese to the butter mixture, in one handful amount, until you achieve your preferred consistency.
4. For the pulled pork, first rub olive oil all over the meat.
5. Rub the BBQ seasoning all over and into the pork shoulder to cover.
6. Place the should on the smoker and cook for 3 hours. After which, spritz the meat with 1 cup of pineapple juice and ½ teaspoon of BBQ rub. Continue with this process every 60 minutes.
7. When the pork shoulder registers an internal temperature of 160°F (70°C) take it out of the smoke and wrap it with a double layer of aluminum foil. Before tightly sealing the foil, pour over ½ cup of pineapple juice.
8. Continue cooking the pork until it registers an internal temperature of 205°F (100°C). Once it does, remove it from the smoker and place in a cooler along with some tea towels. Rest the pork in the cooker for a minimum of 1½ hours before shredding.
9. Serve the pulled pork with a side of cheesy sauce.

PORK CHOPS

INGREDIENTS FOR 4 SERVINGS

THE MEAT

- 4 pork chops 1-in (1-cm) thick

THE RUB

- Black pepper – 1 tablespoon
- Paprika – 1 tablespoon
- Brown sugar – 1 tablespoon
- Kosher salt – 1½ teaspoons
- Dry mustard – ½ teaspoon
- Cayenne pepper – ¼ teaspoon

THE SMOKE

- Set the smoker to 225°F (105°C)
- Add your choice of wood chips to the wood tray

METHOD

1. In a bowl, combine the rub ingredients (black pepper, paprika, brown sugar, kosher salt, dry mustard, and cayenne pepper).
2. Pat the pork chops dry with a kitchen paper towel and scatter the rub generously over the meat, patting it in. Set the pork chops to one side at room temperature for 30 minutes.
3. Place the chops directly on the grate and cook for around 1 hour 15 minutes, or until the meat registers an internal temperature of 145°F (60°C).
4. Halfway through the cooking progress, turn the chops over.
5. Remove from the smoker and allow to rest for 5 minutes before enjoying.

APPLE SMOKED PORK TENDERLOIN

INGREDIENTS FOR 4-6 SERVINGS

THE MEAT

- 2 pork tenderloins (2-lbs, 0.9-kgs) each

THE MARINADE

- Runny honey, warm – 3 tablespoons
- Fresh apple juice – ½ cup
- Pork rub, store-bought, of choice – 3 tablespoons
- Brown sugar – ¼ cup
- Thyme leaves – 2 tablespoons
- Freshly ground black pepper – ½ teaspoon

THE SMOKE

- When you are ready to cook, preheat your smoker to 225°F (110°C) for 12-15 minutes
- Applewood wood chips are recommended for this recipe

METHOD

1. For the marinade: In a bowl, combine the honey, apple juice, pork rub, brown sugar, thyme, and black pepper, and whisk well to incorporate.
2. Add the pork tenderloins to the marinade, turning until evenly and well coat. Cover the bowl with plastic wrap and transfer to the refrigerator for 2-3 hours to marinate.
3. Place the meat directly on the grate and smoke until the pork registers an internal temperature of 145°F (65°C) for 2½-3 hours.
4. Set aside for 6-8 minutes before slicing.
5. Enjoy.

BABY BACK RIBS

INGREDIENTS FOR 4-6 SERVINGS

THE MEAT

- Baby back pork ribs (3-lb, 1.4-kg)

THE INGREDIENTS

- Chili powder – 1 tablespoon
- Ground cumin – 1 tablespoon
- Paprika - 1 tablespoon
- Salt and black pepper, to season
- BBQ sauce of choice – 1 cup

METHOD

1. First, create a rub. Combine the chili powder, cumin, paprika, salt, and black in a bowl.
2. Use a small, sharp knife to cut away the membrane from each rib, then season them all over with the prepared rub.
3. Arrange the ribs on the preheated grill on a higher rack. You can arrange a disposable aluminum tray beneath them to catch any drips.
4. Cook the rubs for 1 hour without lifting the lid at all.
5. Take the ribs off the grill and brush them generously with BBQ sauce. Return the ribs to the grill for 5 more minutes.
6. Serve and enjoy.

JERK PORK SKEWERS

TOTAL COOK TIME 1 HOUR 5 MINUTES

INGREDIENTS FOR 4 SERVINGS

THE MEAT

- Pork fillet, cubed (1-lb, 0.5-kg)
- 8 wooden skewers

THE INGREDIENTS

- Chili sauce – 1 tablespoon
- Ground allspice – 1 teaspoon
- Jerk seasoning – 2 tablespoons
- Olive oil - 1 tablespoon
- 1 small pineapple, peeled and cubed
- Cooked white rice, to serve
- Fresh lime wedges, to serve

METHOD

1. Combine the chili sauce, allspice, and jerk seasoning in a bowl.
2. Add the pork to a large bowl and pour over the jerk mixture. Toss the pork in the mixture to coat evenly. Set aside to marinate for half an hour.
3. In the meantime, soak wooden skewers in water for 20 minutes.
4. Take the soaked skewers out of the water and brush with olive oil.
5. Thread the pork cubes onto the prepared skewers alternating with cubes of pineapple.
6. Place the skewers on the hot grill and cook for 3 minutes on each side until charred and cooked through.
7. Take the skewers off the grill and serve with cooked white rice and garnish with wedges of fresh lime.

PORK CHOPS AND POTATOES

INGREDIENTS FOR 4 SERVINGS

THE MEAT

- 4 pork chops

THE INGREDIENTS

- Olive oil – 2 tablespoons
- Salt and black pepper to taste
- Butter – 2 tablespoons
- Seasoned bread crumbs – 2 cups
- Water – ¾ cup
- 3 medium-size potatoes, cubed
- 1 can cream of mushroom soup (15-ozs, 425-gms)

METHOD

1. Over a campfire, heat the Dutch oven.
2. Add the oil to the Dutch oven.
3. Season the pork chops with salt and black pepper.
4. Once the oil is hot, gently brown the chops.
5. In a separate pan, melt the butter.
6. In a mixing bowl, combine the butter with the breadcrumbs along with ¼ cup of water.
7. Spoon the mixture evenly over the chops, turning them to coat.
8. Add the cubed potatoes on top of the chop mixture.
9. Mix the soup with the remaining ½ cup of water and pour it over the top of the mixture.
10. Assemble the coals under the Dutch oven and on top of the Dutch oven's lid and cook for 60 minutes at 350°F (180°C).
11. Enjoy.

CAMPFIRE CHILI

TOTAL COOK TIME 3 HOURS 45 MINUTES

INGREDIENTS FOR 8-10 SERVINGS

THE MEAT

- Pork shoulder, cut into 2-ins (5.08-cm) chunks (3-lbs, 1.35-kgs)
- Chorizo sausage, raw, and casing removed (1-lb, 0.5-kgs)

THE INGREDIENTS

- Vegetable oil – 2 tablespoons
- 1 large-size onion, peeled and finely chopped
- 1 jalapeno chili, finely chopped
- Chili powder – 3 tablespoons
- Ground cumin – 1 tablespoon
- Dried oregano – 2 teaspoons
- Cilantro, finely minced – 1 cup
- Cannellini beans, soaked in water for 4-6 hours, rinsed and drained
- 2 cans crushed tomatoes (15-ozs, 425-gms) each
- Water
- Kosher salt and freshly ground black pepper
- Scallions, finely sliced – ½ cup

METHOD

1. First, prepare your campfire for cooking.
2. In a Dutch oven, heat the oil over the hot coals until smoking.
3. Add half of the pork shoulder and cook for approximately 10 minutes, until well-browned all over.
4. Transfer the meat to a large-size bowl and repeat the process with the remaining pork. Transfer the second batch to the bowl along with the first batch.
5. Add the chorizo to the pot and cook while breaking up with the back of a wooden spoon until the meat is no longer raw.
6. Return the pork to the pot with the chorizo along with the onion, jalapeno, chili powder, cumin, oregano, and half of the cilantro. Cook while continually stirring for 4 minutes, until the onions are beginning to soften.
7. Next, add the soaked cannellini beans, tomatoes, and sufficient water to cover both the meat and beans by 2-ins (5-cms). Add a large pinch salt.
8. Put the lid on the Dutch oven and cover the lid with hot coals. Allow to heat for 10 minutes. Using long-handled BBQ tongs, check that the liquid is gently bubbling.
9. Cook the beans until soft and creamy, and the pork fork-tender. This will take between 3-6 hours. Timings depend on the cooking heat. For best results, cook low and slow. You will need to check on the chili as it cooks every hour, topping up the water as needed.

SMOKED LEG OF LAMB

CHAPTER 3

LAMB

SMOKED LEG OF LAMB

INGREDIENTS FOR 8 SERVINGS

THE MEAT

- Leg of lamb, excess fat trimmed, silverskin removed (6-lb, 2.7-kg)
- Yellow mustard – 2 tablespoons

THE DRY RUB

- Kosher salt– 1 tablespoon
- Black pepper – 2 teaspoons
- Granulated garlic – 1 teaspoon
- Rosemary – 1 teaspoon
- Thyme – 1 teaspoon
- Brown sugar – 1 teaspoon
- Paprika – ½ teaspoon

THE SMOKE

- Set the smoker to 250°F (120°C)
- You will need 2 pieces of fruit flavored wood for this recipe

METHOD

1. Combine all the rub ingredients in a bowl, breaking up any lumps with a fork.
2. Rub a fine layer of yellow mustard over the lamb.
3. Scatter the rub over the mustard, making sure it is evenly covered.
4. Transfer the lamb to the smoker, and smoke for 4 hours, or until the meat registers an internal temperature of 150°F (65°C).
5. Remove the lamb from the smoker and allow to rest for 10 minutes before slicing.
6. Serve and enjoy

PULLED LAMB SHOULDER

PULLED LAMB SHOULDER

TOTAL COOK TIME 6 HOURS 20 MINUTES

INGREDIENTS FOR 10-12 SERVINGS

THE MEAT

- 1 bone-in lamb shoulder (10-lbs, 4.5-kgs)

THE INGREDIENTS

- Packed dark brown sugar – ¾ cup
- Kosher salt – ½ cup
- Ground espresso beans – ½ cup
- Cracked black pepper – 2 tablespoons
- Garlic powder – 2 teaspoons
- Ground cinnamon – 1 tablespoon
- Ground cumin – 1 tablespoon
- Cayenne pepper – 1 tablespoon
- Hamburger buns, to serve
- Worcestershire sauce – ½ cup
- Stout – ½ cup
- White vinegar – ½ cup
- Ketchup – 1 tablespoon
- Freshly squeezed lemon juice – 2 teaspoons
- Dark brown sugar – 3 tablespoons
- Kosher salt – 1 teaspoon
- Cracked black pepper – ½ teaspoon
- Ground allspice – ¼ teaspoons
- Onion powder – ¼ teaspoon
- Garlic powder – ¼ teaspoon

THE SMOKER

- Add wood chips of your choise to the wood tray
- Preheat the smoker to 225°F (110°C)

METHOD

1. Place the lamb on a rimmed baking pan and put to one side.
2. For the rub: In a bowl, combine the sugar with the salt, espresso beans, pepper, garlic powder, cinnamon, cumin and cayenne and stir thoroughly to incorporate. Aim to yield 2 cups.
3. Use around half of the rub to all the lamb all over. Make sure you rub it into all the meat crevices. Set the remaining rub to one side.
4. Put the lamb in the smoker and smoke at between 225°-250°F (110°-120°C). You may need to replenish the wood chips as necessary.
5. After 4 hours of smoking, check on the lamb's progress every 20 minutes. The lamb is sufficiently cooked when it registers 185°F (85°C) when using an internal thermometer. This will take around 6 hours.
6. Transfer the lamb to a clean rimmed sheet pan and put to one side to rest.
7. In the meantime, prepare the sauce. In a pan over moderate heat, combine 1 ½ cups of water with the remaining ingredients (Worcestershire sauce, stout, vinegar, ketchup, lemon juice, brown sugar, kosher salt, black pepper, allspice, onion powder, and garlic powder). Stir well to incorporate.
8. Bring the sauce to boil before reducing the heat and allowing it to slightly thicken, for 5-7 minutes. Remove the pan from the heat and set aside to cool.
9. Using kitchen tongs, pull the lamb apart while removing and discarding any larger pieces of fat.
10. Once all the lamb has been pulled, add additional rub to taste, and stir well to incorporate.
11. Serve with the hamburger buns and serve the sauce on the side.

HARISSA LAMB CHOPS

INGREDIENTS FOR 4 SERVINGS

THE MEAT

- 8 lamb loin chops on the bone, fat trimmed away

THE INGREDIENTS

- Fresh lemon juice – 2 tablespoons
- Ground cumin – ¾ teaspoon
- 4 garlic cloves, peeled and crushed
- Harissa – 2 tablespoons
- Kosher salt and black pepper, to season
- Olive oil, to grease

METHOD

1. Add the lamb chops to a large bowl and squeeze over fresh lemon juice. Next, add the cumin, crushed garlic, harissa, and a pinch each of salt and black pepper.
2. Cover the bowl with plastic wrap and marinate for an hour.
3. Brush the grill rack with olive oil.
4. Place the lamb chops on the grill and cook for 5 minutes on each side or until the internal temperature registers 145°F (60°C).
5. Take the chops off the grill and allow to rest for a few minutes before serving.

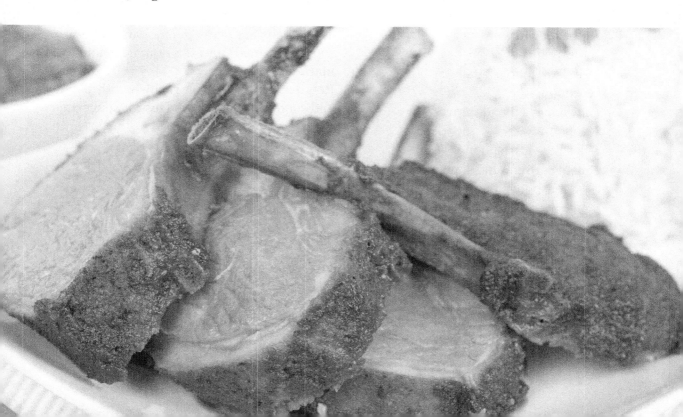

MEDITERRANEAN-STYLE LAMB AND ARTICHOKE KEBABS

TOPIC: GRILLING **TOTAL COOK TIME 1 HOUR 30 MINUTES**

INGREDIENTS FOR 12 SERVINGS

THE MEAT

- Leg of lamb, boneless, fat, and sinew trimmed cut into 1-in (2.5-cms) chunks
- Frozen, quartered artichoke hearts, thawed (12-ozs, 340-gms)
- Parsley, chopped, to garnish
- Fresh lemon wedges, to serve

THE MARINADE

- Extra-virgin olive oil – ¼ cup
- Zest of 1 large lemon, finely grated
- Freshly squeezed lemon juice – 2 tablespoons
- Red wine vinegar – 2 tablespoons
- Dried oregano – 1½ teaspoons
- Garlic, peeled and minced – 1 teaspoon
- Sea salt – 1 teaspoon
- Freshly ground black pepper – ½ teaspoon

THE OUTDOOR GRILL

- Preheat your outdoor grill for direct cooking to 350-450°F (180-230°C)
- Scrape the grill grates until clean

METHOD

1. In a bowl, combine the 8 marinade ingredients (olive oil through black pepper).
2. Add the lamb to the marinade followed by the thawed artichoke hearts, and turn the meat to evenly and well coat. Cover the bowl, and allow to marinate, while occasionally stirring, at room temperature for 60 minutes.
3. Remove from the marinade, shake off any excess and discard the marinade.
4. Thread the lamb and artichokes onto 12 metal skewers. It is advisable to begin and end with an artichoke heart and a minimum of 2 lamb chunks per skewer.
5. Grill the skewers, with the grill lid closed, for 6-8 minutes while flipping over once. The kebabs are ready to enjoy when they are cooked to medium-rare doneness and well marked.
6. Remove from the grill, garnish with parsley and serve with lemon wedges for squeezing.

LAMB SHANKS

LAMB SHANKS

TOTAL COOK TIME 2 HOURS 10 MINUTES

INGREDIENTS FOR 4 SERVINGS

THE INGREDIENTS

- Nonstick cooking spray
- 2 lamb shanks, bone-in (2.2-lbs, 1-kg) each
- 1 package vegetable recipe, soup/dip mix (1.4-ozs, 40-gms)

METHOD

1. Prepare your campfire for cooking.
2. You will need a 12-ins (30.5-cms) Dutch oven with 12 coals underneath it, and 28 on its lid. The desired cooking temperature is 350°F (180°C). You will need to replenish the coals halfway through cooking.
3. Spritz your Dutch oven with nonstick cooking spray.
4. Lay the shanks side by side in the middle of an aluminum foil sheet.
5. Scatter the soup/dip mix over the meat to evenly cover.
6. Bring the longest ends of the aluminum foil together as if you were wrapping a parcel and securely roll to seal tightly. Seal the shortest ends and wrap the parcel in an additional layer of foil.
7. Place the parcel in the middle of the Dutch oven and bake for 2- 2¼ hours, replenishing coals after 60 minutes.

PAN-FRIED LAMB CHOPS

INGREDIENTS FOR 8 SERVINGS

THE MEAT

- 8 lamb chops

THE INGREDIENTS

- Olive oil, divided – 4 tablespoons
- Fresh rosemary, finely chopped -1 tablespoon
- Kosher salt – 1 teaspoon
- Black pepper – ½ teaspoon
- 3 garlic cloves, peeled and minced

METHOD

1. Combine 3 tablespoons of oil in a bowl with the rosemary, salt, black pepper, and garlic. Coat the lamb chops on both sides with the mixture.
2. Heat a cast-iron skillet over the campfire. Add the remaining olive oil to the skillet and swirl the skillet.
3. Add the lamb chops to the skillet in a single layer and cook for 2-4 minutes, depending on the desired level of doneness.
4. Take the chops out of the skillet and allow to rest for 5 minutes.

CHERRY COLA CHICKEN WINGS

CHAPTER 4

POULTRY

SMOKED CHICKEN LEGS

INGREDIENTS FOR 6 SERVINGS

THE MEAT

- Chicken legs (3-lb, 1.5-kg)

THE INGREDIENTS

- Olive oil – 3 tablespoons
- Poultry dry rub, any brand – as needed

THE SMOKE

- Set the smoker to 250°F (120°C)

TOTAL COOK TIME 2 HOURS 35 MINUTES

METHOD

1. Add the chicken legs to a large ziplock bag.
2. Pour the olive oil into the bag, followed by a liberal amount of dry rub. Using clean hands, make sure the chicken legs are evenly coated. You may need to add more oil if necessary. Allow to rest for a minimum of 60 minutes.
3. Smoke the chicken legs for 1½-2 hours until the internal temperature registers 165°F (75°C).
4. Then preheat your broiler to high heat.
5. Place the chicken in the middle of the oven, skin side facing upwards, and broil for around 3 minutes until the fat crackles but the skin doesn't burn.
6. Enjoy.

CAMPIRE BBQ CHICKEN

INGREDIENTS FOR 4 SERVINGS

THE POULTRY

- 4 large chicken breasts

THE INGREDIENTS

- 6 slices of bacon
- 1 red onion, peeled and chopped
- 6 small potatoes, sliced
- Butter(1-lb, 0.45-kgs)
- 1 bottle BBQ sauce, of choice

TOTAL COOK TIME 1 HOUR 10 MINUTES

METHOD

1. Prepare your campfire for cooking. You will need approximately 24-26 coals.
2. Once the coals are burning, place the Dutch oven on top.
3. Add the bacon to the Dutch oven and cook through. Drain the majority of the bacon dripping, leaving only ¼ cup remaining in the Dutch oven.
4. Next, add the onions followed by the potatoes, chicken, butter, and BBQ sauce.
5. Cover the Dutch oven with its lid while placing 14 coals underneath and 12 on the lid.
6. Cook for approximately 35-50 minutes until the chicken is cooked through.

CHERRY COLA CHICKEN WINGS

INGREDIENTS FOR 12 SERVINGS

THE MEAT

- Chicken wings, partitioned, tips discarded (4-lb, 1.8-kg)

THE BRINE

- Cherry cola – 4¼ cups
- Kosher salt – 2 tablespoons

THE INGREDIENTS

- BBQ rub – 4 tablespoons
- Brown sugar – 4 tablespoons
- Cornstarch – 4 tablespoons

THE SMOKE

- Add your favorite wood chips to the wood tray
- Preheat the smoker to 150°F (65°C)

METHOD

1. Around 18 hours before you cook the wings, add them to a ziplock bag.
2. Pour in the cherry cola and 2 tablespoons of kosher salt.
3. Remove the wings from the brine, and pat dry with kitchen paper.
4. Transfer the wings to a very large bowl.
5. Add the BBQ rub, brown sugar, and cornstarch. Toss until well and evenly covered.
6. Smoke the wings for around 2 hours.
7. Remove from the smoker and enjoy.

CRISPY TURKEY WINGS

INGREDIENTS FOR 4 SERVINGS

THE MEAT

- 1 whole or split turkey wings, patted dry (3-lb, 1.5-kg)

THE INGREDIENTS

- Olive oil – 2 tablespoons
- Brown sugar – 2 teaspoons
- Chili powder – 1 teaspoon
- Onion powder – ½ teaspoon
- Garlic powder – ½ teaspoon
- Smoked paprika – 1 teaspoon
- Salt and black pepper, to season

THE SMOKE

- Set the smoker to 225°F (105°C)

METHOD

1. Drizzle oil over the turkey wings.
2. Add the sugar, chili powder, onion powder, garlic powder, and smoked paprika to a bowl, and stir to combine. Scatter the seasoning over the wings to cover on both sides. Rub the mixture into the turkey wings and season with salt and black pepper.
3. Place the seasoned wings on the smoker and smoke until they reach an internal temperate of 165°F (75°C). This will take around 2 hours.
4. For crispy skin, increase the smoker temperature to 350°F (175°C), and smoke for 15-20 minutes, flipping over, until crisp.
5. Allow to cool before serving.

TURKEY MEATBALLS IN CRANBERRY CHILI SAUCE

INGREDIENTS FOR 8 SERVINGS

THE POULTRY

- 1 package frozen prepared turkey meatballs (2-lbs, 0.9-kgs)

THE INGREDIENTS

- 1 bottle mild chili sauce (12-ozs, 340-gms)
- 1 can cranberry jelly sauce (16-ozs, 450-gms)
- Packed brown sugar – 2 tablespoons
- Freshly squeezed lemon juice – 1 tablespoon

METHOD

1. Prepare your campfire for cooking.
2. In your Dutch oven, combine the mild chili sauce, cranberry sauce with the sugar and freshly squeezed lemon juice. Cook over moderate heat until the sugar dissolves.
3. Add the meatballs, stir to combine and warm through to a temperature of 165°F (75°C) for 20-25 minutes.
4. Serve and enjoy.

WILD TURKEY BREAST

WILD TURKEY BREAST

INGREDIENTS FOR 4-6 SERVINGS

THE MEAT

- Turkey breast, deboned thigh, tied, skin on (2-lbs, 0.9-kg)

THE BRINE

- Brown sugar – 1 cup
- Kosher salt – 2 tablespoons
- Freshly cracked black pepper – 2 tablespoons
- Cold water – 4 cups

THE RUB

- Garlic powder – 2 tablespoons
- Dried onions – 2 tablespoons
- Black pepper – 2 tablespoons
- Brown sugar – 2 tablespoons
- Cayenne pepper – 1 tablespoon
- Chili powder – 2 tablespoons
- Paprika – ¼ cup
- Salt – 1 tablespoon
- Sugar – 2 tablespoons
- Ground cumin – 2 tablespoons

THE SMOKE

- With the lid closed, preheat the smoker to 180°F (82°F)

METHOD

1. First, prepare the brine: In a large-size glass bowl, combine the brown sugar with the salt, cracked pepper, and water.
2. Add the turkey to the brine, weighing down to entirely submerge.
3. Place in the fridge for 12 hours.
4. Take the turkey out of the brine, shake off any excess, and discard the brine.
5. For the rub, in a bowl, combine the garlic powder with the dried onions, black pepper, brown sugar, cayenne, chili powder, paprika, salt, sugar, and cumin.
6. Season the turkey all over with the rub and place the skin side facing upwards directly on the grill grate.
7. Smoke the meat for 5-8 hours, until it registers an internal temperature of 160°F (71°C).
8. Remove the turkey from the smoker and set aside to rest for several minutes, during which time it will continue to cook until it achieves an internal breast temperature of 165°F (75°C).
9. Slice, serve, and enjoy.

LEMONGRASS GRILLED CHICKEN

TOPIC: GRILLING

TOTAL COOK TIME 2 HOURS 15 MINUTES

INGREDIENTS FOR 4 SERVINGS

THE MEAT

- 8 whole skinless, boneless chicken thighs

THE INGREDIENTS

- Lemongrass marinade, store-bought – 1 cup
- 2 red chili pepper, sliced into thin rings, to garnish
- Fresh cilantro leaves to garnish
- Wedges of fresh lemon, to serve

METHOD

1. Add the chicken thighs and store-bought marinade to a ziplock bag. Seal the bag and gently massage to ensure the meat is coated. Transfer to the fridge for 2 hours.
2. Remove the chicken from the bag, and discard the marinade.
3. Grill the chicken at moderately high heat, for 4 minutes on each side, until golden.
4. Remove the chicken from the grill and allow to rest for 5 minutes.
5. Garnish with red chili peppers and cilantro leaves.
6. Serve with wedges of fresh lemon for squeezing.

TEXAS TOAST WITH GRILLED TURKEY BREAST AND BASIL PESTO

TOPIC: GRILLING

INGREDIENTS FOR 8 SERVINGS

THE MEAT

- Turkey breast (10.5-oz, 298-gm)

THE INGREDIENTS

- Salt and black pepper, to taste
- Fresh lemon juice, to taste
- 8 slices Texas toast

THE PESTO

- Fresh basil (3-oz, 85-gm)
- Pine nuts, toasted – ⅓ cup
- 2 garlic cloves, peeled and coarsely chopped
- Fine sea salt – ¼-½ teaspoon
- Lemon juice – 1 tablespoon
- Parmesan cheese, grated – ¼ cup
- Extra virgin olive oil – ½ cup

TOTAL COOK TIME 25 MINUTES

METHOD

1. Add the basil, pine nuts, garlic, salt, lemon juice, and Parmesan to a blender and with the machine running, gradually stream in the oil blend to a creamy soft consistency. Taste and adjust the seasoning with more salt, lemon juice or Parmesan, as needed
2. Grill the turkey breast over high heat, and when cooked through, season with salt, black pepper and lemon juice.
3. Grill the Texas toast.
4. Spread 4 slices of toast with the pesto.
5. Cut the grilled turkey breast into small pieces and top with the remaining slices of toast to create sandwiches.
6. Enjoy.

MEDITERRANEAN - STYLE GRILLED CHICKEN

MEDITERRANEAN-STYLE GRILLED CHICKEN

TOPIC: GRILLING

TOTAL COOK TIME 3 HOURS 20 MINUTES

INGREDIENTS FOR 6 SERVINGS

THE MEAT

- 1 whole chicken, butterflied
- Salt, as needed

THE MARINADE

- Extra virgin olive oil - ⅓ cup
- Fresh juice and zest of 2 lemons
- Dried oregano – 1 tablespoon
- Fresh thyme – 1 tablespoon
- Paprika – 1 teaspoon
- Ground coriander – 1 teaspoon
- Cumin – ½ teaspoon
- Black pepper – ½ teaspoon
- Cayenne pepper – ½ teaspoon
- 12 garlic cloves, peeled and minced

METHOD

1. First, pat the butterflied chicken dry and season with salt all over and under the skin.
2. In a bowl, combine the marinade ingredients (olive oil, lemon juice, lemon zest, dried oregano, thyme, paprika, coriander, cumin, black pepper, cayenne pepper, and garlic cloves).
3. Place the chicken in a large dish with sides. Apply most of the marinade under the chicken skin. Rub the marinade on the back of the chicken also and transfer the chicken to the fridge for 2-4 hours.
4. Lightly oil the grill grates.
5. Place the chicken over indirect heat and with the lid closed, cook at 400°F (200°C) for 45-60 minutes. The chicken is ready when it registers an internal temperature of 165°F (75°C).
6. Remove from the grill and allow to rest for 10 minutes before slicing and serving.

CHEESY CHILI PEPPER AND LIME CHICKEN

INGREDIENTS FOR 4 SERVINGS

THE INGREDIENTS

- Nonstick cooking spray
- 8 skinless, boneless chicken thighs
- Freshly squeezed juice of 2-3 limes
- Taco seasoning – 3 tablespoons
- 8 canned whole green chilies, drained
- Part-skim mozzarella cheese, shredded – 1 cup
- Sour cream, to serve, optional

METHOD

1. Prepare your campfire for cooking.
2. You will need a 10-ins (25.4-cms) Dutch oven with 10 coals in a ring around it and 22 on the lid. You may need to replenish the coals after 30 minutes of cooking. The desired cooking temperature is 400°F (205°C).
3. Spritz the Dutch oven with nonstick cooking spray.
4. Arrange the chicken thighs in your Dutch oven.
5. Squeeze the fresh lime juice over the chicken and season with the taco seasoning.
6. Slice the chilies lengthwise, cutting into, but not right the way through. Open them flat and place 1 on top of each chicken thigh.
7. Bake for 35-40 minutes.
8. Scatter the shredded cheese over the top and bake for another 5-6 minutes until the cheese is melted and gooey.
1. Enjoy with a dollop of sour cream..

MAPLE GLAZED SALMON

PART 2 FISH, SEAFOOD, GAME MEATS

CHAPTER 5

FISH

SINGLE MALT-CURED COLD SMOKED SALMON

TOPIC: SMOKING

TOTAL COOK TIME 40 HOURS

INGREDIENTS FOR 8-10 SERVINGS

THE FISH

- 1 whole fresh salmon fillet, center-cut, skin-on. Total weight (1.5-lb, 0.7-kg)
- Vegetable oil, as needed, for oiling the rack

THE CURE

- Single malt Scotch whiskey– 1 cup
- Packed brown dark sugar – 1 cup
- Coarse sea salt – ½ cup
- Freshly ground black pepper – 1 tablespoon

THE SMOKE

- Set your smoker for cold smoking following the manufacturer's instructions

METHOD

1. Rinse the fish under cold running water, and using kitchen paper, blot dry. Run your fingers over the fleshy side of the salmon, feeling for pin bones or sharp bits, and with kitchen tweezers, remove.
2. To a nonreactive dish, add the salmon.
3. Pour the whiskey over the fish, and cover the dish. Transfer to the fridge for around half an hour, flipping the fish over twice. Using a colander, drain the salmon, discard the whiskey and blot the fish dry with kitchen paper. Clean the baking dish with kitchen paper.
4. Add the dark sugar, salt, and pepper to a bowl, and mix thoroughly while breaking up any lumps with clean fingers.
5. Spread ½ cup of the sugar mixture into the bottom of the baking dish.
6. Place the salmon on top of the sugar mixture, skin side facing down. Scatter over the remaining 1 cup of the cure, using your fingertips to rub it into the fish flesh. Cover with plastic wrap and transfer to the fridge to cure for 24 hours.
7. Remove the salmon from the fridge, and rinse under cold running water. Blot the fish dry with kitchen paper towels.
8. Set an oiled rack over a rimmed baking sheet.
9. Place the salmon skin side facing down on the oiled rack and allow to air dry in the fridge, uncovered until a pellicle forms, for around 2 hours.
10. Transfer the fish on the rack to the smoker, and smoke for 12-18 hours until the fish is golden and the edges are firm. The smoker's temperature should be below 80°F (30°C).
11. Transfer the salmon on its rack to a rimmed baking sheet and set aside to cool to room temperature. Transfer to the fridge, wrapped in foil, until you are ready to serve. The salmon can be stored in the refrigerator for a minimum of 72 hours.
12. When you are ready to serve, slice the salmon on the diagonal and enjoy.

HALIBUT IN PARCHMENT

HALIBUT IN PARCHMENT

INGREDIENTS FOR 4-6 SERVINGS

THE FISH

- 4 halibut fillets, boned (4-ozs, 115-gms) each

THE INGREDIENTS

- Kosher salt and freshly ground black pepper
- Olive oil
- 2 Meyer lemons ends trimmed, cut into 12 even slices
- Corn kernels from 2 ears of corn
- 16 asparagus spears, sliced ½ -ins (1.30-cms) thick
- Assorted mixed herbs, finely chopped – 2 tablespoons

THE SMOKE

- Preheat your smoker to high heat, with the lid closed for 12-15 minutes
- We recommend alder wood for this recipe

METHOD

1. First, cut 4 sheets of parchment paper, each one 18-ins (46-cms) long.
2. Arrange one fillet of fish in the middle of each sheet—season with a pinch of salt and a dash of pepper. Drizzle with oil. Put 3 slices of fresh lemon on each fillet, slightly overlapping them to cover the halibut.
3. Scatter ¼ each of corn kernels, and asparagus around the halibut. Drizzle with oil and season.
4. Take the longer sides of the parchment paper and bring them together. Fold the top edges of the paper down to create a 1-ins (2.54-cms) seal. Continue to tightly fold down over the halibut and veggies. In opposite directions, twist the open ends of the paper. This will prevent any steam escaping.
5. Repeat the assembly process until all the parcels are prepared.
6. Place the parcel on a baking sheet.
7. Transfer the sheet to the smoker and bake for 15 minutes until the parcels are browned and puffed, and the fish flakes easily when using a fork.
8. Remove the parcels from the smoker and set aside to rest for 4-5 minutes.
9. Using scissors, cut an X-shape into the middle of each parcel, pull back the paper, and garnish with herbs.
10. Serve.

ALBACORE TUNA

INGREDIENTS FOR 4 SERVINGS

THE FISH

- 4 albacore tuna steaks (6-oz, 170-gm) each and 1-in (2.55-cm) thick

THE INGREDIENTS

- Extra virgin olive oil – 3 tablespoons
- Salt and black pepper, to season
- Freshly squeezed juice of 1 lime

METHOD

1. Add the tuna steaks to a large ziplock bag along with the olive oil. Seal well, and transfer to the fridge for 60 minutes.
2. Preheat your grill to moderate heat, and if using a smoker grill, presoak ½ cup of mesquite or hickory wood chips.
3. Lightly oil the grill grate.
4. Season the fish with salt and black pepper, and cook on the preheated grill for 6 minutes, flipping it over once.
5. Transfer the fish to a platter, and drizzle with lime juice.
6. Enjoy.

MAPLE GLAZED SALMON

INGREDIENTS FOR 4 SERVINGS

THE FISH

- Salmon fillet (2-lb, 0.9-kg)

THE GLAZE

- Real maple syrup – ¼ cup
- Worcestershire sauce – 1 tablespoon
- Granulated garlic – 1 teaspoon
- Coarse ground pepper – 1 teaspoon
- Dry mustard – ½ teaspoon

METHOD

1. Whisk the maple syrup with Worcestershire sauce, garlic, ground pepper, and mustard in a bowl.
2. If you are using a smoker grill, pecan pellets are a good choice for this recipe.
3. Place the salmon on the grill and, over indirect heat, cook the fish, skin side down at 325°F (165°C).
4. Brush the glaze all over the fish in a thick and even layer. Close the grill lid and cook for 5 minutes.
5. Add a second layer of glaze over the fish, and continue grilling into the fish registers an internal temperature of 145°F (65°C).
6. Remove the salmon from the heat, transfer to a baking sheet and set aside to rest for 5 minutes before serving.

CHEESY SHRIMP STUFFED TROUT

TOTAL COOK TIME 35 MINUTES

INGREDIENTS FOR 4 SERVINGS

THE FISH

- 4 trout fillets

THE INGREDIENTS

- Olive oil
- Onion, peeled and diced – ¼ cup
- Celery, chopped – ¼ cup
- Bread, cubed – 2 cups
- Monterey Jack cheese, shredded – ¼ cup
- Canned baby shrimp, cooked – ½ cup
- Parsley, chopped – 3 tablespoons

METHOD

1. Prepare your campfire for cooking. Allow the fire to burn down until the coals are red, with white ashes around the edges.
2. Lightly oil a 13-ins (33-cms) Dutch oven.
3. In your Dutch oven, sauté the onion along with the celery.
4. Add the cubed bread and gently toss.
5. Next, add the shredded cheese, followed by the canned shrimp and parsley.
6. Lightly season the cavity of the fish and stuff with the bread mixture.
7. Brush the fish lightly with butter and season.
8. Cove with a lid.
9. Place 10-12 coals underneath and 16-18 coals on the lid of the oven.
10. You will need to check the cooking progress. You can do this by gently lifting the lid using long-handled tongs. Cook until the fish flakes easily when using a fork. The fish is sufficiently cooked when it registers an internal heat of 145°F (63 °C). This will take between 7-10 minutes, depending on the heat of the campfire.
11. Serve and enjoy.

WHITE FISH BREAD BAKE

INGREDIENTS FOR 4 SERVINGS

TOTAL COOK TIME 50 MINUTES

THE INGREDIENTS

- Nonstick cooking spray
- Stale bread, torn into small pieces – 5 cups
- 2 garlic cloves, peeled and finely diced
- 3 sprigs curly parsley, finely chopped
- White fish, of choice (2.2-lbs, 1-kg)
- Salt and black pepper, to season
- Olive oil – ½ cup
- Butter, cut into cubes – 3 tablespoons

METHOD

1. Prepare your campfire for cooking.
2. You will need a 12-ins (30.5-cms) Dutch oven sprayed with nonstick cooking spray. Place 9 coals underneath it and 18 on its lid. The desired cooking temperature is 350°F (180°C).
3. Add the torn bread, garlic, and parsley to a bowl and mix well to combine.
4. Add half of the bread mixture to the prepared Dutch oven, and flatten.
5. Lay the fish on top of the bread and season with salt and black pepper.
6. Drizzle the oil over the top and dot with cubes of butter.
7. Bake for 40-50 minutes or until the fish flakes easily when using a fork.
8. Serve and enjoy.

SMOKED OYSTERS WITH COMPOUND BACON BUTTER

CHAPTER 6

SEAFOOD

SHRIMP AND PESTO LINGUINE

TOPIC: SMOKING   **TOTAL COOK TIME 45 MINS**

INGREDIENTS FOR 4 SERVINGS

THE SEAFOOD

- Fresh shrimp, peeled and deveined (1-lb, 0.5-kg)

THE INGREDIENTS

- Oil, divided – 3 tablespoons
- Dried oregano – 1 tablespoon
- Garlic powder – 1 teaspoon
- Salt – 1 teaspoon
- 1 red pepper, cored and diced
- A bunch of asparagus, chopped into 4 pieces
- Pesto, store-bought – ½ cup
- Parmesan cheese, freshly grated - ⅓ cup
- Linguini pasta, cooked al dente, drained (1-lb, 0.5-kg)

THE SMOKE

- Preheat your smoker to 225°F (110°C)
- Alder, apple, and cherry wood chips are good choices for this recipe

METHOD

1. Add the shrimp to a bowl, and toss with 2 tablespoons of oil, oregano, garlic powder, and salt. Arrange the shrimp on the smoker racks.
2. Smoke the shrimp until they are cooked through and become pink. This step will take around 30-45 minutes.
3. Add the remaining oil to a skillet over moderate heat. Add the red pepper and asparagus and cook while frequently stirring until the veggies are cooked.
4. Stir in the pesto and Parmesan cheese and take the pan off the heat.
5. Toss the al dente pasta with the shrimp, and red pepper, and asparagus mixture.
6. Enjoy.

SMOKED OYSTERS WITH COMPOUND BACON- BUTTER

TOPIC: SMOKING   **TOTAL COOK TIME 1 HOUR 5 MINUTES**

INGREDIENTS FOR 4 SERVINGS

THE SEAFOOD

- 24 fresh whole oysters, shucked

THE INGREDIENTS

- 2 rashers of smoked bacon, cut in half
- Butter, room temperature – ½ cup
- 2 garlic cloves, peeled and minced
- Fresh parsley, minced – 1 tablespoon
- 4 lemon wedges, to serve

THE SMOKE

- Add a combination of white wine and water to the water bowl
- Add applewood wood chips to the tray
- Preheat the smoker to 225°F (110°C) with the top vent open and the door closed

METHOD

1. Over moderate to high heat, heat a frying pan or skillet.
2. Add 4 bacon halves to the pan and cook until crisp. Remove the bacon from the pan and place on a plate lined with kitchen paper to drain.
3. Add the butter to a bowl.
4. Crumble the crisp bacon and add it to the butter, followed by the garlic.
5. With a fork, stir in the parsley.
6. Place the bacon butter on a piece of kitchen wrap and form into a log-shape approximately 1-ins (2.5-cms) in diameter.
7. Roll the butter in the wrap tightly and from into a cylindrical-shape. Twist the ends tightly.
8. Transfer the compound butter to the freezer until cold enough to slice into coins.
9. Place the shucked oysters on a sheet tray, taking care not to overcrowd the oysters or spill any of their liquid.
10. Remove the butter from the freezer.
11. Unwrap the butter and into coins 0.25-ins (0.65-cms) thick.
12. Place a butter coin on top of each of the oysters.
13. Transfer the sheet tray(s) to the smoker and smoke for half an hour until they are smoky and their edges curled. If they are not cooked to this level, return to the smoker and smoke in 15-minute intervals. Take care, though, not to over-smoke and dry the oysters out.
14. Serve with wedges of fresh lemon.

GRILLED LOBSTER TAIL

GRILLED LOBSTER TAIL

INGREDIENTS FOR 4 SERVINGS

THE SEAFOOD

- 4 lobster tails (10-oz, 280-gm) each

THE INGREDIENTS

- Butter, melted – 5 tablespoons
- Fresh lemon juice – 1 tablespoon
- Fresh parsley, chopped – 2 tablespoons
- Fresh basil, chopped – 2 tablespoons
- 3 garlic cloves, peeled and minced
- Salt, to season
- Wedges of fresh lemon, for serving

METHOD

1. In a bowl, whisk the melted butter with fresh lemon juice, parsley, basil, garlic and salt to season. Put aside.
2. Using kitchen shears, cut along the center of the top of the lobster tail towards the tail fins, taking care not to cut through the fin. With your fingers, open up the shell gently.
3. Using kitchen shears, cut halfway through the lobster meat down the middle, again taking care not to cut all the way through.
4. Insert a metal skewer through the lobster lengthwise.
5. Brush the lobster meat lightly with the butter mixture.
6. Grill the lobster, meat side down, for around 5-6 minutes, or until charred lightly.
7. Flip the lobster over, brush with the remaining butter and grill for another 4-5 minutes, until it is cooked through and opaque.
8. Remove the lobster from the grill.
9. Garnish the lobster with wedges of lemon for squeezing.

GRILLED CRAB LEGS

INGREDIENTS FOR 4 SERVINGS

THE SEAFOOD

- Frozen king or snow crab legs, thawed (4-lb, 1.8-kg)

THE INGREDIENTS

- Nonstick olive oil spray
- Wedges of fresh lemon, for squeezing
- Butter, melted, for dipping

METHOD

1. Spritz the crab legs all over with nonstick cooking spray.
2. Place the crab legs on a hot grill.
3. Cover and grill for around 7 minutes on each side, or until the crab meat is heated through.
4. Cut slits along the sides with a sharp knife to make it easy to pull out the meat.
5. Remove the lobster meats to plates and serve with wedges of fresh lemon and melted butter.

BEER-STEAMED CLAMS

INGREDIENTS FOR 4 SERVINGS

THE INGREDIENTS

- Butter – 2-3 tablespoons
- Fresh Manila clams (2-lbs, 0.9-kgs)
- 1 can pale lager
- 1 lemon, cut into 4 wedges
- 8 garlic cloves, peeled and minced

METHOD

1. Prepare your campfire.
2. In a Dutch oven, melt the butter over moderate heat and add the clams, lager, lemon, and garlic.
3. Cover with a lid, and steam for approximately 6-8 minutes or until they open. Remove and discard any unopened clams.
4. Serve and enjoy.

ASIAN SHRIMP

ASIAN SHRIMP

INGREDIENTS FOR 4 SERVINGS

THE SEAFOOD

- Large shrimp, tails off, peeled and deveined (1-lb, 0.5-kgs)

THE INGREDIENTS

- Water – 4 tablespoons
- Soy sauce – 1 tablespoon
- Sugar- 1 teaspoon
- Vegetable oil – 2 tablespoons
- One small onion, peeled and thinly sliced
- Four garlic cloves, peeled and finely chopped
- Four green onions, whites and greens chopped
- Mushrooms, sliced (4-ozs, 141.75-gms)
- 1 jalapeno pepper, seeded and finely chopped
- 1 cup loosely packed fresh basil, rolled into cigar shapes and thinly cut into strips
- Rice, cooked

METHOD

1. Prepare your campfire for cooking using either coals or charcoal briquettes.
2. In a bowl, combine the water with the soy sauce and sugar. Stir well and put to one side.
3. Over moderately high heat, preheat your Dutch oven over the campfire coals.
4. Add the oil to the Dutch oven.
5. Stir in the shrimp and cook for a few minutes before adding the onion, garlic, greens onions, mushrooms, and jalapeno pepper. Stir well until just softened. Take care not to overcook the shrimp before adding the other ingredients.
6. Pour in the sauce set aside earlier and stir well until sufficiently heated through. The shrimp are ready when they are slightly opaque, and the flesh is white. It is recommended that the internal temperature of seafood should register 145°F (65°C) when using a meat thermometer.
7. Remove from the heat and stir in the basil.
8. Serve with rice and enjoy.

BISON BRISKET

CHAPTER 7

WILD GAME

GOOSE BRACIOLE

GOOSE BRACIOLE

INGREDIENTS FOR 4 SERVINGS

THE MEAT

- 2 boneless, skinless goose breasts

THE INGREDIENTS

- Granulated garlic powder – 1 teaspoon
- Basil pesto, store-bought – ½ cup
- 4 slices prosciutto
- 4 bacon slices
- Olive oil – 1 tablespoon

THE SMOKE

- Set the smoker to 375°F (190°C) with the lid closed for 15 minutes

METHOD

1. Place the goose breasts on a chopping board. Take a knife, hold it horizontally to the board, then make a cut along the middle side and cut all the way through to yield 4 pieces. Pound the breast portions to flatten.
2. Next, season the flattened goose with granulated garlic powder. Spread a thin layer of basil pesto over the breasts and top each one with a slice of prosciutto.
3. Beginning on one side, roll the goose up and then wrap it with a slice of bacon. Secure the bacon using kitchen twine and drizzle with olive oil. Set aside and continue with the remaining goose pieces.
4. Place the wrapped goose on the smoker's grill grates, close the smoker's lid, and cook for 10 minutes.
5. Flip the goose oven and cook for another 10 minutes.
6. Remove the heat and put aside to rest for 19 minutes.
7. Remove the kitchen twine, slice, serve and enjoy.

SMOKED WILD GAME SAUSAGES

TOTAL COOK TIME 13 HOURS 15 MINUTES

INGREDIENTS FOR 4-6 SERVINGS

THE MEAT

- Wild boar, ground (½-lb, 0.20-kgs)
- Venison, ground (½-lb, 0.20-kgs)

THE INGREDIENTS

- Fast cure salt – 1½ teaspoons
- Mustard seeds – ½ teaspoon
- Black pepper – ½ teaspoon
- Garlic powder – ½ teaspoon

THE SMOKE

- Start your smoker with the lid open to establish the fire; this will take between 4-6 minutes. Preheat the temperature to 225°F (110°C).
- Preheat with the lid closed for 12-15 minutes.

METHOD

1. Add the wild boar, venison, fast cure salt, mustard seeds, black pepper and garlic powder to a bowl, and mix to combine. Take care not to over mix as this causes the sausages to be tough. Transfer the mixture to the fridge, overnight.
2. Using clean hands, form the mixture into a log shape and wrap in kitchen wrap.
3. Twist the ends of the plastic wrap tightly and smooth out the log.
4. Slowly and carefully unwrap the log to maintain its even shape.
5. Place the log directly on the heated smoker grate and smoke for between 3-4 hours. Remove from the smoker and allow to cool for 60 minutes, at room temperature.
6. Enjoy.

BISON BRISKET

INGREDIENTS FOR 4 SERVINGS

THE MEAT

- Bison brisket (3-lb, 1.5-kg)

THE INGREDIENTS

- Kosher salt and black pepper, as needed, to season
- Dark red ale, any brand, quantity as needed
- BBQ sauce, any brand, quantity as needed
- Chicken stock, quantity as needed
- Olive oil, as needed

THE SMOKE

- Set the smoker to 200°F (95°C) for indirect heat

METHOD

1. Generously season the meat on all sides with salt and black pepper. Transfer to the fridge for 48 hours before smoking.
2. Once you are ready to begin smoking, lay the meat on the smoker's rack and smoke for 2 hours.
3. When 2 hours have elapsed, the meat should have an internal temperature of around 120°F (50°C). Then, coat the meat all over with oil. Smoke for another 30 minutes.
4. Drizzle ale and BBQ sauce over the meat, followed by chicken stock.
5. With pink butcher paper, wrap the bison brisket.
6. Place the meat in a foil tray and return to the smoker. You will need to check every 60 minutes to ensure enough liquid exists to keep the meat moist.
7. After 4½ hours, increase the smoker's temperature to 240°F (110°C). Continue checking on the meat's smoking process every 60 minutes, adding more liquid as needed.
8. When 12-14 hours have elapsed, and the meat has reached an internal temperature of around 200°F (95°C), remove from the smoker. Cover the tray and meat wrapped tightly with foil and allow to cool for 60 minutes before slicing.
9. Enjoy.

GRILLED QUAIL

GRILLED QUAIL

INGREDIENTS FOR 3-4 SERVINGS

THE MEAT

- 8 semi-boneless quail (rib cage removed)

THE INGREDIENTS

- Dijon mustard – 1 tablespoon
- 2 garlic cloves, peeled
- Mixed herbs, rosemary, sage and thyme, chopped – 2 tablespoons
- Freshly squeezed lemon juice – 3 tablespoons
- Kosher salt – 1 teaspoon
- Black pepper – ½ teaspoon
- Olive oil - ⅓ cup

METHOD

1. Cut the quail in half and place it in a shallow baking dish.
2. Whisk the mustard with garlic, mixed herbs, and fresh lemon juice in a small bowl. Season with 1 teaspoon of kosher salt and ½ teaspoon of black pepper. Drizzle the oil slowly into the mixture until combined. Pour the vinaigrette over the quail, and flip them over to coat. Cover and transfer to the fridge to marinate for 2-6 hours.
3. Brush the grill grates with oil, and set up your grill for direct-heat cooking over moderately high heat.
4. Remove the quail from the marinade, and scrape off any excess.
5. Smooth the skin out, and season the bird with salt and black pepper.
6. Lay the quail on the grill with the skin side facing down, and cook for 3-5 minutes on each side.
7. Remove the quail from the grill and allow to rest for 5 minutes.
8. Serve hot and enjoy.

GRILLED CORNISH HENS

TOPIC: GRILLING

TOTAL COOK TIME 1 HOUR 5 MINUTES

INGREDIENTS FOR 4 SERVINGS

THE MEAT

- 4 Cornish game hens. Total weight (1.25-lb, 0.60-kg)

THE INGREDIENTS

- Butter, softened – ¼ cup
- 2 green onions, finely chopped
- Fresh parsley, minced – 2 tablespoons
- Fresh ginger root, minced – 2 tablespoons
- 3 garlic cloves, peeled and minced
- Salt, divided – 1 teaspoon
- Black pepper, divided – ½ teaspoon

METHOD

1. Combine the butter, green onions, parsley, ginger, garlic, ½ teaspoon salt, and ¼ teaspoon black pepper in a bowl.
2. Rub the butter mixture until the bird's skin and over the surface. Scatter over the remaining salt and pepper and season inside the cavities.
3. With long-handled kitchen tongs, moisten a kitchen paper towel with cooking oil and coat the grill rack. Next, prepare your grill for indirect heat using a drip pan.
4. Place the Cornish hens, breast side up over the drip pan, and while covered, grill over moderate indirect heat for 45-60 minutes, until the internal temperature of the meat registers 180°F (80°C).
5. Serve and enjoy.

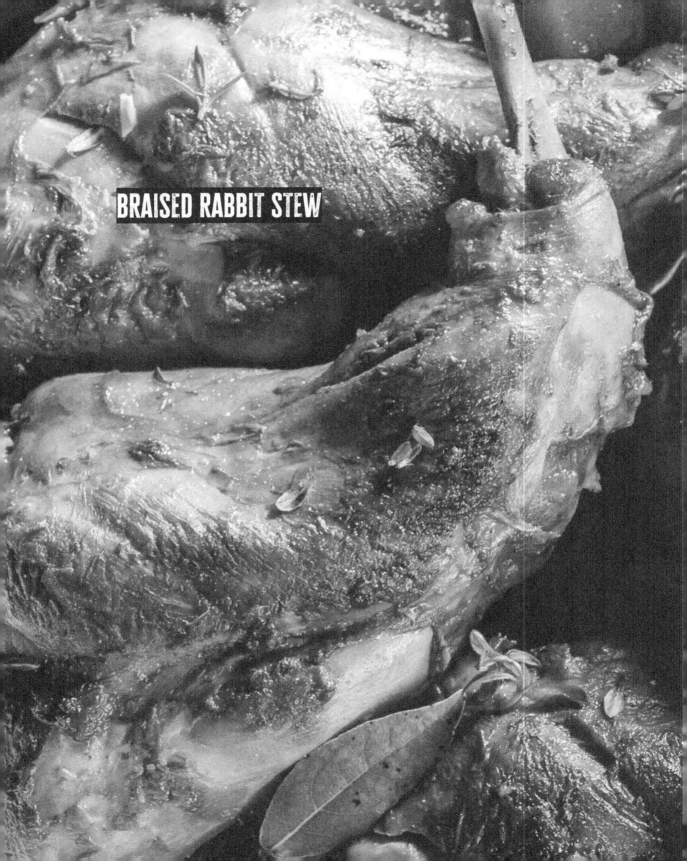

BRAISED RABBIT STEW

BRAISED RABBIT STEW

TOTAL COOK TIME 2 HOURS 30 MINUTES

INGREDIENTS FOR 4-6 SERVINGS

THE MEAT

- Rabbit dressed and cut up (3-lbs, 1.4-kgs)

THE INGREDIENTS

- Butter – 2 tablespoons
- 1 yellow onion, peeled and chopped
- 1 carrot, peeled and chopped
- 1 celery stalk, chopped
- 2 garlic cloves, peeled and chopped
- Flour – 2 tablespoons
- Red wine – 1 cup
- Chicken stock – 4 cups
- 2 bay leaves
- Sprig of thyme

METHOD

1. Prepare your campfire for cooking using either coals or charcoal briquettes.
2. Heat 1 tablespoon of butter over moderate to high heat
3. Once the oil is hot, in batches, browns the pieces of rabbit until golden. Set to one side.
4. Add 1 tablespoon of butter and once melted, add the onion along with the carrot and celery. Sauté for 10 minutes, until the carrots are fork-tender and the onions, translucent. Next, add the garlic and sauté for an additional 60 seconds.
5. Scatter the flour over the onion mixture and stir thoroughly, cooking for an additional 60 seconds. While stirring, add the wine along with the stock.
6. Return the rabbit to the pan, making sure they are 75 percent covered in the liquid.
7. Add the bay leaves and thyme and bring to simmer.
8. Cook the meat for 2 hours until tender and pulling easily off the bone.

HOT MEXICAN-STYLE BEEF JERKY

PART 3 JERKY, VEGGIES, DESSERTS, SAUCES

CHAPTER 8

JERKY

HOT MEXICAN-STYLE BEEF JERKY

TOPIC: SMOKING

TOTAL COOK TIME 13 HOURS 25 MINUTES

INGREDIENTS FOR 8-12 SERVINGS

THE MEAT

- Flank steak beef, partially frozen, cut into ¼-ins (0.64-cms) strips (2-lbs, 0.9-kgs)

THE MARINADE

- 1-2 jalapenos, stemmed, with seeds
- Soy sauce – ¼ cup
- Freshly squeezed lime juice – ¼ cup
- Brown sugar – 4 tablespoons
- Quick curing salt – 1 tablespoon
- Mexican lager beer – 1 cup

METHOD

1. To prepare the marinade: Add the jalapenos, soy sauce, fresh lime juice, brown sugar and curing salt to a food blender, and process until the pepper is finely chopped.
2. Pour the mixture into a large bowl and stir in the Mexican beer.
3. Add the slices of beef to a large ziplock bag.
4. Pour the marinade over the beef and gently massage to evenly and entirely coat. Seal the bag and transfer to the fridge, overnight.
5. When you are ready to cook, with the lid of your grill set on smoke, establish the fire, for 4-5 minutes.
6. Take the slices of beef out of the marinade and shake off any excess marinade.
7. Place the beef in between two layers of kitchen paper and pat dry.
8. Remove the beef from the towels, and in a single layer, arrange directly onto the grill grate.
9. Smoke the jerky until it is dry, chewy and pliable. This will take between 4-5 hours.
10. Transfer the warm jerky to a ziplock bag and set aside to rest at room temperature for 60 minutes.
11. Squeeze out any excess air from the bag and place in the fridge for up to 6 weeks.
12. Enjoy.

TUNA JERKY

INGREDIENTS FOR 6 SERVINGS

THE FISH

- Tuna fillets, cut into thin strips (2-lbs, 0.9-kgs)

THE BRINE

- Soy sauce – 2 cups
- Runny honey – 3 tablespoons
- Sambal Oelek Indonesian seasoning – 3 tablespoons

THE SMOKE

- While the smoker is cold, add peach wood chips to the tray
- Set the smoker to 200°F (95°C)

METHOD

1. Add the soy sauce to a small microwave-safe bowl, and in the microwave, heat for 1-2 minutes.
2. Stir in the honey and Sambal Oelek seasoning until the honey dissolves entirely. Set the brine aside to cool.
3. Add the tuna strips to a glass bowl.
4. Pour the cooled brine over the strip and place in the fridge for 2 hours.
5. Remove the tuna from the fridge, and place on a wire rack. Return to the fridge uncovered to dry out for 1-2 hours.
6. Smoke the tuna strip in the smoker until firm yet pliable, for 3-4 hours.
7. Remove from the smoker, set aside to cool entirely before enjoying.

RABBIT JERKY

RABBIT JERKY

INGREDIENTS FOR 8-12 SERVINGS

THE MEAT

- Belly flaps from 10 rabbits, fat trimmed, cut into jerky-size slices

THE MARINADE

- Freshly squeezed orange juice – 1 cup
- Soy sauce – 1 cup
- Honey – ½ cup
- Black pepper – 1 tablespoon
- Cayenne pepper – 1 teaspoon
- Fresh ginger, grated – 1 teaspoon
- Pink curing salt – ½ teaspoon

THE SMOKER

- Preheat your smoker to 160°F (70°C)
- Mesquite or hickory wood chips are recommended for this recipe

METHOD

1. In a glass bowl, combine the orange juice with the soy sauce, honey, black pepper, cayenne pepper, grated ginger, and pink curing salt.
2. Add the rabbit and stir thoroughly to evenly and well coat. Set aside to marinate for 4-8 hours.
3. Dry the rabbit jerky in your dehydrator set at 160°F (70°C), on low in the oven with the door cracked open a few inches, or in your smoker until flexible, but dry. This will take approximately 5-6 hours.

LAMB JERKY

INGREDIENTS FOR 12-20 SERVINGS

THE MEAT

- Lamb fillets – (1-lb, 0.5-kgs)

THE INGREDIENTS

- Onion salt – 1 tablespoon
- Liquid smoke – 2 tablespoons
- Soy sauce – 4 tablespoons
- Worcestershire sauce - ⅓ cup
- Hickory seasoning liquid – 1½ teaspoons
- 5-6 drops of Tabasco sauce

THE SMOKE

- Preheat the smoker to 160-180°F (70-80°C)
- Mesquite or hickory wood chips are recommended for this recipe

METHOD

1. Cut the lamb into 0.25-ins (0.5-cms) strips.
2. Combine the onion salt with the liquid smoke, soy sauce, Worcestershire sauce, hickory seasoning liquid, and Tabasco sauce. Add to a ziplock bag along with the strips of lamb. Seal the bag and transfer to the fridge for 6-24 hours.
3. Remove the meat from the ziplock bag. Smoke the jerky until it is dry, chewy, and pliable. This will take between 4-6 hours.
4. Remove the jerky from the smoker and set aside to rest at room temperature.
5. Enjoy.

VENISON JERKY

INGREDIENTS FOR 6- 8 SERVINGS

THE GAME

- Venison, trimmed (2-lb, 0.90-kgs)

THE MARINADE

- Apple cider vinegar – 1 teaspoon
- Granulated garlic – 1 teaspoon
- Salt – 1 teaspoon
- Soy sauce – ½ cup
- Worcestershire sauce – ½ cup
- Brown sugar – 1 tablespoon
- White pepper – 2 teaspoons
- Ground cloves – 1 teaspoon
- Ground cinnamon – 2 teaspoons
- Star anise – 2 teaspoons
- Ground nutmeg – 1 teaspoon

THE SMOKE

- When you are ready to beginning cooking, with the lid open, on smoke start your grill to establish the fire, this will take 4-6 minutes.

METHOD

1. Using a sharp kitchen knife, slice the venison into ¼-ins (0.63-cms) thick slices. Remove any fat or connective tissue.
2. Add the marinade ingredients to a bowl (apple cider vinegar, granulated garlic, salt, soy sauce, Worcestershire sauce, brown sugar, white pepper, ground cloves, and cinnamon) and whisk to combine.
3. Transfer the mixture to a Ziploc bag and securely seal, expelling as much air from the bag as possible. Transfer to the fridge, overnight.
4. Remove the venison from the bag and shake off any excess marinade. Discard the marinade.
5. In a single layer, arrange the venison directly on the heated grill grate. Season with a little more pepper, cloves, cinnamon, star anise, and nutmeg.
6. Smoke until the jerky is dry but chewy and slightly bendy; this will take between 4-5 hours.
7. Remove the jerky from the grill and transfer to a wire rack to cool for 60 minutes.
8. Store in the fridge in a Ziploc bag.

SMOKED JALAPENOS

CHAPTER 9

VEGGIES

BUTTER SMOKED CABBAGE

INGREDIENTS FOR 4-6 SERVINGS

THE VEGETABLES

- 1 cabbage

THE INGREDIENTS

- Irish salted butter – ½ cup
- All-purpose rub – 2 tablespoons
- White balsamic vinegar – 2 tablespoons
- Freshly ground black pepper, to season

THE SMOKE

- Preheat the smoker to 250°F (120°C)

METHOD

1. First, core the cabbage and put 1 large size leaf to one side.
2. Rub the butter, in layers, inside the core until it is filled. Season all over with all-purpose rub. Using your finger, make a well shape inside the butter.
3. Pour the vinegar into the well to fill.
4. Place the large cabbage leaf over the top to secure.
5. Smoke for 4 hours before removing from the smoker, wrapping in aluminum foil, and continue to smoke for 2 hours, until your preferred level of tenderness.
6. Season with black pepper and serve.

SMOKED JALAPENOS

INGREDIENTS FOR 15-20 SERVINGS

THE INGREDIENTS

- Large, ripe jalapenos (2-lb, 0.9-kg)

THE SMOKE

- Set the smoker to 250°F (120°C)
- Use pecan or apple wood chips for this recipe

TOTAL COOK TIME 4 HOURS 5 MINUTES

METHOD

1. Place the jalapenos along with their stems, seeds and membranes rack in a single layer, a little apart on a smoker rack or tray. Close the lid and smoke the jalapenos. Place the peppers on the hotspot, as this will avoid you having to move them around.
2. Smoke for 4 hours, checking their progress every 60 minutes. They are ready when they are blackened and dark and appear leather-like.
3. Remove from the smoker and enjoy.

GRILLED ZUCCHINI WITH ASIAN STYLE SAUCE

INGREDIENTS FOR 4 SERVINGS

THE SAUCE

- Reduced-sodium soy sauce
- Sesame oil – 3 tablespoons
- 4 garlic cloves, peeled and finely minced
- Sugar – 1 tablespoon

THE INGREDIENTS

- 2-3 zucchini, sliced into 12 thick strips approximately 0.25-in (0.64-cm) thick
- Olive oil, for grill grates
- Toasted sesame seeds, to garnish – 1 tablespoon
- Red pepper flakes, to garnish

TOTAL COOK TIME 20 MINUTES

METHOD

1. In a pan over moderate heat, combine the soy sauce with sesame oil, garlic, and sugar, whisk to combine and while frequently stirring, bring to a simmer until the mixture starts to thicken. Remove the pan from the heat, and put aside.
2. Place the zucchini strips in a single layer on an oil greased grill grate and grill over moderately high heat, with the grill lid closed, for 3 minutes.
3. Using tongs, turn the zucchini over, cover with the grill lid and cook until tender and charged, for 2-3 minutes.
4. Remove the zucchini from the grill and brush with the soy sauce mixture.
5. Garnish with sesame seeds and red pepper flakes, and serve.

CARROT DOGS

INGREDIENTS FOR 6 SERVINGS

THE MARINADE

- Black pepper – ½ teaspoon
- Garlic, peeled and minced – 1 teaspoon
- Ground coriander – ¼ teaspoon
- Ground cinnamon – ¼ teaspoon
- Ground cumin – ½ teaspoon
- Ground nutmeg – ¼ teaspoon
- Paprika – ½ teaspoon
- Allspice – ¼ teaspoon
- Olive oil ½ cup
- Liquid aminos – 6 tablespoons

THE INGREDIENTS

- 6 carrots, trimmed, peeled
- ½ white onion, peeled and sliced
- ½ red bell pepper, cut into strips
- 6 hot dog buns, split
- Ketchup, mustard, or condiment of choice, to serve

METHOD

1. In a bowl, combine the marinade ingredients (black pepper, garlic, coriander, cinnamon, cumin, nutmeg, paprika, allspice, olive oil, and liquid aminos).
2. Trim the carrots lengthwise into a hot dog shape.
3. Add the chopped carrots to the marinade and marinate overnight.
4. When you are ready to cook, remove the carrots from the marinade, and grill on moderate heat of around 350°F (180°C) until charred slightly.
5. Add the onion and red peppers to the grill.
6. Toast the buns.
7. Build the toasted buns with carrot dogs, veggies and your favorite condiment.

CHICKPEA AND VEGGIE HANS

CHICKPEA AND VEGGIE HASH

TOTAL COOK TIME 20 MINUTES

INGREDIENTS FOR 2 SERVINGS

THE INGREDIENTS

- Oil – 1 tablespoon
- 1 small red onion, peeled and sliced into half-moons, 0.25-in (0.64-cm)
- 1 zucchini, sliced into half-moons, 0.5-in (1.27-cm)
- 3 mini sweet peppers, cut into slices, 0.25-in (0.64-cm)
- 1 can chickpeas, drained (15-oz, 425.2-gm)
- Cumin – ½ teaspoon
- Coriander – ¼ teaspoon
- Ground cinnamon - ⅛ teaspoon
- Salt – ½ teaspoon
- 2 eggs

METHOD

1. Heat the oil in a cast-iron skillet until it shimmers.
2. Add the red onions, zucchini, sweet peppers, and saute for 5 minutes until they start to soften.
3. Then add the chickpeas, cumin, coriander, cinnamon, and salt, and cook for around 10 minutes, until the chickpeas and veggies are browned in spots and cooked through.
4. Push the chickpeas and veggies to the sides of the skillet. Make a well-shape in the center of the pan. If the bottom of the pan is looking a little dry, add a splash of oil.
5. Crack the eggs into the well and cook to your preferred level of doneness.
6. Enjoy.

HONEY CORNBREAD WITH CHEESE AND GREEN CHILIES

TOPIC: CAST IRON CAMPING   **TOTAL COOK TIME 30 MINUTES**

INGREDIENTS FOR 6 SERVINGS

THE INGREDIENTS

- Nonstick cooking spray
- Whole milk – 1 cup
- 1 medium egg
- Runny honey – 2 tablespoons
- Cornmeal – 1 cup
- Flour – ½ cup
- Baking powder – 1 tablespoon
- Salt – 1 teaspoon
- Butter – 2 tablespoons
- 1 can green chilies, drained (4-ozs, 113.4-gms)
- Cheddar cheese, grated– ¼ cup

METHOD

1. Prepare your campfire for cooking.
2. You will need a 12-ins (30.5-cms) Dutch oven with 7 coals underneath it in a ring and 17 on its lid.
3. Spritz the Dutch oven with nonstick cooking spray.
4. In a bowl, beat the milk with the egg and honey.
5. To the bowl, for the batter, add the cornmeal, flour, baking powder, and salt, stirring thoroughly to incorporate.
6. Add the butter to the hot Dutch oven and melt.
7. When the butter has melted, add the batter.
8. Sprinkle the chilies and grated cheese over the batter.
9. Cover. Add the coals to the lid and cook for 20-25 minutes until the middle of the cornbread is cooked and the top is gently browned.
10. Serve and enjoy.

SEA SALTED CARAMEL MERINGUES

CHAPTER 10

DESSERTS AND SAUCES

BBQ BAKED FIGS WITH HONEY

TOPIC: BARBECUE **TOTAL COOK TIME 15 MINUTES**

INGREDIENTS FOR 4 SERVINGS

THE INGREDIENTS

- 8 ripe figs, stemmed
- Clean runny honey – 3 tablespoons
- Knob of butter, diced
- Ground cinnamon
- Pistachio nuts, coarsely chopped, to serve
- Ice cream, to serve

METHOD

1. Make a deep X-shape in each fig, taking care to stop before the base.
2. Squeeze the figs gently at their bases, to open them up like a flower.
3. Put the figs into an enamel or heatproof dish and drizzle over the runny honey.
4. Dot the butter, around and on top of the figs, and scatter over the ground cinnamon.
5. Place the dish on the BBQ, away from the direct heat. Close the lid and cook for 8-10 minutes, until the figs are softened.
6. Take the figs out of the BBQ and allow to cool.
7. Scatter the pistachios over the top and serve with ice cream

SEA SALTED CARAMEL MERINGUES

TOPIC: BARBECUE

TOTAL COOK TIME 1 HOUR 30 MINUTES

INGREDIENTS FOR 10-12 SERVINGS

THE INGREDIENTS

- 2 egg whites, at room temperature
- Caster sugar – ½ cup
- White vinegar – ½ teaspoon
- Vanilla extract – ½ teaspoon
- Caramel sauce, store-bought – 3 teaspoons
- Sea salt flakes

METHOD

1. Using a stand mixer, beat the egg whites until stiff peaks start to form.
2. Add the sugar gradually and beat for 30 seconds between each addition.
3. When all of the sugar is added, beat for another 6-8 seconds, until the whites are glossy and thick.
4. Preheat your BBQ for low and slow cooking.
5. To the egg whites, add the vinegar and vanilla, beating thoroughly until incorporated.
6. Line a baking tray with baking paper.
7. Using a teaspoon, add the caramel topping to a piping bag.
8. Next, add the meringue to the bag.
9. Using a star nozzle, pipe the mixture into 2-ozs (5.08-cms) rounds onto the baking paper. Make sure you leave enough space between the rounds to allow for spreading.
10. Scatter sea salt over the meringues.
11. Place the baking tray of meringues on the BBQ and bake slow and on low heat for 35-40 minutes, until crisp. You may need to adjust the burner heat on the right to achieve 285°F (140°C).
12. Once the meringues are crisp, remove from the BBQ and set aside to cool for 30-40 minutes.

GRILLED PEARS WITH CINNAMON HONEY AND PECANS

GRILLED PEARS WITH CINNAMON HONEY AND PECANS

TOPIC: GRILLING

TOTAL COOK TIME 40 MINUTES

INGREDIENTS FOR 3-6 SERVINGS

THE INGREDIENTS

- 3 bosc pears, halved and deseeded
- Coconut oil, melted – 1 tablespoon
- Pinch sea salt
- Honey – 2 tablespoons
- Ground cinnamon – 1 tablespoon
- Chopped pecans – ¼ cup

METHOD

1. Preheat your grill to 350-400°F (180-205°C).
2. Brush the pear halves evenly with melted coconut oil and sprinkle with a pinch of sea salt.
3. Place the pears on the grill, cut side facing down, and cook for 15 minutes until the pears are soft and have distinct grill marks. Turn the pears at a 45° angle and grill for another 10-15 minutes to create diamond-shaped char marks.
4. Take the cooked pears off the grill and allow to rest for 10 minutes.
5. When ready to serve, stir together the honey and cinnamon in a small bowl.
6. Drizzle the cinnamon honey over the warm pears and scatter over the pecans. Serve straight away.

GRILLED CHERRY AND OAT COBBLER

INGREDIENTS FOR 10 SERVINGS

THE INGREDIENTS

- Nonstick cooking spray
- Frozen sweet dark cherries, pitted - 4 cups
- Fresh lemon juice – 1 tablespoon
- Granulated sugar – ¼ cup
- Whole-wheat flour – ½ cup
- Old-fashioned oats – ½ cup
- Light brown sugar – ¼ cup
- Ground cinnamon – ¼ teaspoon
- Unsalted butter, at room temperature – ¼ cup

METHOD

1. Preheat the grill to 350-400°F (180- 205°C) and spritz a large-sized cast iron skillet with nonstick cooking spray.
2. In a bowl, toss together the cherries, lemon juice, and sugar until combined. Pour the mixture into the skillet.
3. In a second bowl, stir together the flour, oats, sugar, and cinnamon. Using clean hands, rub the butter into the dry ingredients until combined and crumbly. Scatter the mixture over the cherries in the skillet.
4. Cover the skillet with foil and place on the grill, close the grill lid, and cook for 20 minutes. Discard the foil and continue to grill for 10 more minutes until the cherry mixture is bubbling and the topping is golden.
5. Take the skillet off the grill and allow to cool for 10-15 minutes before serving.

DUTCH BABY WITH BERRIES

TOTAL COOK TIME 45 MINUTES

INGREDIENTS FOR 6 SERVINGS

THE INGREDIENTS

- 9 eggs
- Whole milk – 1½ cups
- Vanilla extract – 1 tablespoon
- Zest of 1 lemon
- Flour – 1½ cups
- Salt – ½ teaspoon
- Butter – ½ cup
- Berries, of choice – 4 cups
- Confectioner's sugar – ¼ cup
- Freshly squeezed lemon juice, to serve, optional

METHOD

1. Prepare your campfire for cooking.
2. When you are ready to begin cooking, prepare a 12-ins (30.5-cms) Dutch oven. You will need 14 coals on the top of the Dutch oven lid and 7 around it. You may need to replenish the coals after 30 minutes of baking.
3. In a bowl, combine the eggs with the milk, vanilla extract, and lemon zest. When you are ready to cook the Dutch Baby, add the flour and the salt and whisk well until blended.
4. Once the coals are good and hot, place 8 coals under the Dutch oven. Add a cube of butter to the pan and melt. When melted, add the batter and cover with a lid. Place 16 coals on top of the lid.
5. Every 5 minutes, rotate the lid a ¼ turn and cook until set, for approximately 25 minutes. It will puff up to the lid but fall back down when the lid is taken off.
6. Remove the Dutch oven from the heat.
7. Cover with berries, a dusting of confectioner's sugar, and a squeeze of fresh lemon juice. Place the lid back on the Dutch oven and warm the berries before serving.
8. Slice into 6 portions and enjoy.

MISSISSIPPI MUD CAKE

TOPIC: CAST IRON CAMPING

TOTAL COOK TIME 50 MINUTES

INGREDIENTS FOR 6 SERVINGS

THE INGREDIENTS

- All-purpose flour – 2 cups
- Sugar – 1½ cups
- Baking powder – 1 tablespoon
- Cocoa powder – ½ cup
- Brown sugar – 2 cups
- Ground cinnamon – 1 teaspoon
- Non-fat dairy milk – ½ cup
- Water – ¾ cup
- Oil – ½ cup
- 3 eggs
- Water, hot – 1 cup
- Vanilla extract, divided – 3 teaspoons
- Semi-sweet chocolate chips (10-ozs, 283.5-gms)
- Pecans, chopped – ¾ cup

METHOD

1. When you are ready to begin cooking, prepare 22-26 coals. Using heavy foil, line the bottom and sides of a 12-ins (30.5-cms) Dutch oven.
2. In a ziplock bag, combine the dry ingredients (flour, sugar, and baking powder).
3. Mix the dry ingredients for the mud (cocoa powder, brown sugar, and cinnamon) in a second ziplock bag.
4. For the cake, add the remaining cake ingredients (water, oil, eggs and 1 teaspoon of vanilla extract) the dry cake mix from Step 2. Pour the mixture into the Dutch oven.
5. In the same bowl, mix the dry mix from Step 3 with the hot water and remaining vanilla extract. Pour the mud mixture over the cake batter.
6. Cover the Dutch oven with its lid and bake with 8-10 briquettes on the bottom and 14-16 briquettes on the Dutch oven's lid. Bake for 45 minutes or until the cake is set. You will need to rotate the Dutch oven and lid every 10-15 minutes.
7. Once the cake is ready, scatter over the chocolate chips and chopped pecans, cover with a lid, and allow to melt for approximately 4-6 minutes.
8. Serve warm and enjoy.

LEMON BUTTER SAUCE

LEMON BUTTER SAUCE
TOTAL TIME 5 MINUTES

INGREDIENTS FOR ⅓ CUP

THE INGREDIENTS

- Unsalted butter, chopped into pieces – ¼ cup
- 1 garlic clove, peeled and grated
- Sea salt – ¼ teaspoon
- Freshly squeezed lemon juice – 2 tablespoons
- Freshly ground black pepper, to season
- Fresh parsley, chopped, to garnish
- A pinch of red pepper flakes, to serve, optional

METHOD

1. Over low heat, and in a small pan, melt the butter.
2. Add the garlic and salt to the pan and cook for 60 seconds.
3. Take the pan off the heat, and add the fresh lemon juice. Season with pepper and sprinkle over the chopped parsley and red pepper flakes.
4. Serve the sauce with fish, over pasta or rice.

MUSTARD-ORANGE RUB
TOTAL TIME 10 MINUTES

INGREDIENTS FOR 18 SERVINGS

THE INGREDIENTS

- Dijon mustard – 2 cups
- Fresh parsley, minced – 1 cup
- Dried orange peel – ½ cup
- Rosemary leaves, crushed – ½ cup
- Black pepper – ¼ cup
- Salt – 1 tablespoon

METHOD

1. Combine the mustard, parsley, orange peel, rosemary leaves, black pepper, and salt.
2. Use as directed.

PEACH BARBECUE GLAZE
TOTAL TIME 45 MINUTES

INGREDIENTS FOR 4 CUPS

THE INGREDIENTS

- 4 ripe peaches, peeled, pitted, and pureed
- White vinegar – 1 cup
- Vegetable oil – ¼ cup
- 1 garlic cloves, peeled and crushed
- Freshly squeezed lemon juice – 3 tablespoons
- Worcestershire sauce – 1 tablespoon
- Ground ginger – ¼ teaspoon
- Black pepper – ½ teaspoon
- Dijon mustard – 1 tablespoon
- Corn syrup – ¾ cup
- Ground cinnamon – 1 teaspoon
- Light brown sugar – 1 cup

METHOD

1. In a large pan, combine the peach puree with the white vinegar, vegetable oil, garlic, lemon juice. Worcestershire sauce, ground ginger, black pepper, mustard, corn syrup, cinnamon, and light brown sugar. Heat the mixture to a low boil, and continue to simmer while frequently stirring for 30 minutes.
2. Use the glaze to baste pork, chicken, or ham.

PEANUT AND GINGER MARINADE
TOTAL COOK TIME 20 MINUTES

INGREDIENTS FOR 2 CUPS
THE INGREDIENTS

- Hot water – ½ cup
- Smooth peanut butter – ½ cup
- Chili paste – ¼ cup
- Soy sauce – ¼ cup
- White vinegar – 2 tablespoons
- Vegetable oil – 2 tablespoons
- 4 garlic cloves, peeled and minced
- Red pepper flakes – ¼ teaspoon
- Small chunk fresh ginger, grated

METHOD

1. In a bowl, stir together the hot water and peanut butter until the peanut butter has melted. Next, stir in the chili paste, soy sauce, vinegar, vegetable oil, garlic, red pepper flakes, and ginger.
2. Add your choice of meat to the marinade and toss to coat. Cover and chill overnight before cooking.

SWEET AND SPICY APRICOT BASTING SAUCE
TOTAL TIME 20 MINUTES

INGREDIENTS FOR 2 CUPS
THE INGREDIENTS

- Apricot jam – 1 cup
- White vinegar – ½ cup
- Worcestershire sauce – 3 tablespoons
- Dijon mustard – 2 tablespoons
- Honey – 2 tablespoons
- Crushed red pepper – 2 teaspoons

METHOD

1. In a small pan, combine the apricot jam, white vinegar, Worcestershire sauce, Dijon mustard, honey, and red pepper. Heat over moderate heat until the jam and honey melt.
2. Brush the baste over the meat at the end of the grilling process.

RED WINE SAUCE

MOROCCAN-STYLE MARINADE
TOTAL TIME 5 MINUTES

INGREDIENTS FOR ⅗ CUP

THE INGREDIENTS

- 2 garlic cloves, peeled
- Rose harissa – 1 tablespoon
- Ground cumin – 1 teaspoon
- Ground coriander – 1 teaspoon
- Freshly squeezed lemon juice – 1 tablespoon
- Olive oil – 3 tablespoons
- Runny honey – 1 teaspoon
- Flaked sea salt – ½ teaspoon
- Coarsely ground black pepper to season

METHOD

1. Flatten the garlic cloves and place in a bowl with the end of a rolling pin.
2. Add the rose harissa, cumin, coriander, fresh lemon juice, olive oil, honey, sea salt, and a liberal amount of black pepper to the bowl. Stir well to combine.
3. Use as needed.

HONEY SOY BASTE FOR PORK CHOPS
TOTAL TIME 15 MINUTES

INGREDIENTS FOR ⅛ CUP

THE INGREDIENTS

- Honey – 1 tablespoon
- Dijon mustard – 1 tablespoon
- Soy sauce – 1 tablespoon
- 1 garlic clove, peeled and minced

METHOD

1. Combine the honey, Dijon mustard, soy sauce, and garlic in a small bowl. Stir to incorporate.
2. Use the baste for pork chops while basting frequently.
3. This recipe is enough for 4 pork chops.

DUCK CURE

DUCK CURE

INGREDIENTS FOR 1¼ CUPS

THE INGREDIENTS

- Brown sugar (3.5-oz, 100-gm)
- Coarse salt (4.6-oz, 130-gm)
- Sichuan peppercorns, crushed – 2 teaspoons
- Fennel seeds, crushed – 1 teaspoon

METHOD

1. Combine the brown sugar, coarse salt, Sichuan peppercorns, and fennel seeds in a bowl.
2. To use, spread around ⅓ of the cure in the bottom of a dish that is a snug fit for the duck. Place the duck fillet skin side facing up and completely cover the remaining cure. Cover with kitchen wrap and transfer to the fridge for 72 hours.
3. Use as directed in your recipe.

RED WINE SAUCE

TOTAL TIME 15 MINUTES

INGREDIENTS FOR 1⅝ CUPS

THE INGREDIENTS

- Red wine – 1 cup
- Butter – ½ cup
- Poultry seasoning – ¼ teaspoon
- Garlic powder – ¼ teaspoon
- A pinch of ground sage
- Freshly squeezed lemon juice – 2 tablespoons
- Hot pepper sauce, any brand, as needed

METHOD

1. Over moderate heat, in a pan, combine the red wine with butter, poultry seasoning, garlic powder, sage, fresh lemon juice, and a few dashes of hot pepper sauce, to taste. Stir thoroughly until blended. Simmer the sauce for approximately 10 minutes.
2. Serve and enjoy.

CAROLINA MOPPING SAUCE

CHERRY BBQ SAUCE

TOTAL TIME 25 MINUTES

INGREDIENTS FOR 3½ CUPS

THE INGREDIENTS

- Fresh sweet cherries, stemmed and pitted – 2 cups
- Water, divided - ⅔ cup + 1 tablespoon
- Brown sugar – ½ cup
- Tomato paste – 1 tablespoon
- Balsamic vinegar – 3 tablespoons
- Garlic, peeled and minced – 1 teaspoon
- Salt
- A pinch of red chili flakes
- Cornstarch – 1 tablespoon

METHOD

1. Combine the cherries, ⅔ cup water, sugar, tomato paste, balsamic vinegar, garlic, salt, and red pepper flakes in a pot. Over moderate to high heat, bring to a boil. Turn the heat down to moderate heat and simmer until the fruit is softened and the sauce is reduced slightly. This step will take around 10 minutes.

2. Using an immersion blender, puree the cherries. Strain the puree through a fine-mesh strainer and remove and discard the skins.

3. Return the puree to the pot and bring to a simmer over moderate heat.

4. In a small bowl, combine the cornstarch with one tablespoon of water. Whisk the slurry a little at a time into the sauce until you achieve your preferred consistency.

5. Allow the sauce to cool and store in a suitable container in the fridge for no more than 3 weeks.

6. Serve with chicken or pork.

CAROLINA MOPPING SAUCE

TOTAL TIME 10 MINUTES

INGREDIENTS FOR 16 SERVINGS

- Distilled white vinegar – 1 cup
- Cider vinegar – 1 cup
- Red pepper flakes – 1 tablespoon
- Hot sauce – 1 tablespoon
- Garlic powder – 1 teaspoon
- Onion powder – 1 teaspoon
- Packed brown sugar – 2 tablespoons
- Dry mustard – 1 teaspoon
- Salt – ½ teaspoon
- Ground black pepper – ¼ teaspoon

METHOD

1. Combine the white vinegar, cider vinegar, red pepper flakes, hot sauce, garlic powder, onion powder, brown sugar, dry mustard, salt, and black pepper in a bowl.
2. Transfer to an airtight resealable container and store in the fridge for up to 28 days.
3. Use as directed.

LIME MARINADE FOR SALMON

TOTAL TIME 1 HOUR

INGREDIENTS FOR 1 CUP

THE INGREDIENTS

- Pure honey - 5 tablespoons
- Zest of 1 fresh lime
- Freshly squeezed lime juice – 2 tablespoons
- Cornstarch – 1 teaspoon
- Sriracha – 1 teaspoons

METHOD

1. Over moderate heat, in a small pan, combine the honey with the lime zest, lime juice, cornstarch, and Sriracha, until the cornstarch is dissolved entirely. When no bits of gritty cornstarch remain, turn the heat to moderate-high. Continue to whisk and simmer for approximately 60 minutes until thickened.
2. Remove the pan from the heat, cover with a lid and keep the glaze warm. Use as needed.

VERY BERRY BBQ SAUCE FOR RIBS
TOTAL TIME 30 MINUTES

INGREDIENTS FOR 6 CUPS
THE INGREDIENTS

- Fresh blueberries – 2 cups
- Fresh blackberries – 2 cups
- Sugar – ½ cup
- Water – ¼ cup
- BBQ sauce, store-bought, of choice – 1-2 cups

METHOD

1. In a pan, combine the blueberries, blackberries, sugar, and water, and bring to a boil. Turn the heat down, and uncovered, simmer until thickened for 15-20 minutes. You will need to occasionally stir the mixture during this process.
2. Stir in your preferred amount of BBQ sauce, and cook until thickened for an additional 10-15 minutes.
3. Store the sauce in a suitable airtight container in the fridge for no more than 72 hours.

SPICY LEMONGRASS
TOTAL TIME 4 MINUTES

INGREDIENTS FOR ⅓- ½ CUP
THE INGREDIENTS

- 2 fresh lemongrass stalks, bottom 5-ins (12.7-cms) of inner bulb only, finely sliced
- Fresh ginger, peeled and chopped – ¼ cup
- 1 medium jalapeno pepper, halved
- Vegetable oil – 2 tablespoons
- Cilantro leaves – 2 tablespoons
- Salt, as needed

METHOD

1. In a food processor, combine the lemongrass with ginger, garlic, and jalapeno. On the pulse setting, finely chop. Add the oil and process to a coarse paste consistency.
2. Next, add the cilantro leaves and process until smooth.
3. Season the rub liberally with salt.
4. Use the rub for lean fish, chicken, seafood, beef, or pork. It is also suitable for stirring into ground turkey, chicken, or pork for burgers, meatloaf, or meatballs.
5. Store the wet rub in a suitable container in the fridge for no more than 72 hours.

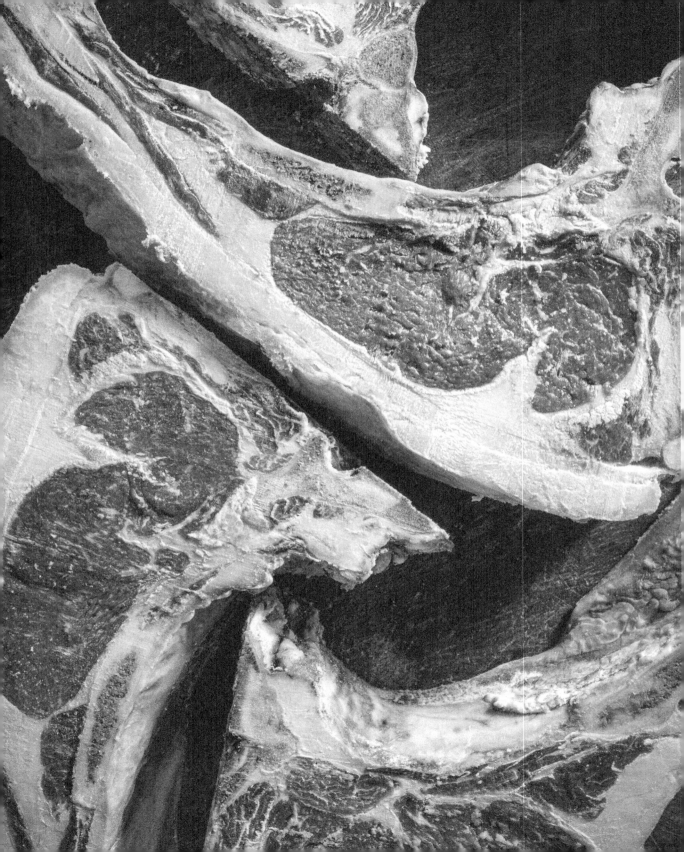

PART 4 🔪 BASICS AND FOOD SAFETY

CHAPTER 11 BARBECUING AND SMOKING MEAT

CHAPTER 12 CAMPING

CHAPTER 13 FOOD SAFETY

CHAPTER 11
BARBECUING AND SMOKING MEAT

You might not believe it, but there are still people who think that the process of Barbequing and Smoking are the same! So, this is something you should know about before diving deeper. So, whenever you use a traditional BBQ grill, you always put your meat directly on top of the heat source for a brief amount of time which eventually cooks up the meal. Smoking, on the other hand, will require you to combine the heat from your grill as well as the smoke to infuse a delicious smoky texture and flavor into your meat. As a result, smoking usually takes much longer than traditional barbecuing. In most cases, it takes a minimum of 2 hours and a temperature of 100 -120 degrees for the smoke to be properly infused into the meat. Keep in mind that the time and temperature will depend on the type of meat you are using, which is why it is suggested to keep a meat thermometer handy to ensure that your meat is doing fine. Also, remember that this barbecuing method is also known as "Low and slow" smoking. With that cleared up, you should be aware that there are two different ways smoking is done.

COLD AND HOT SMOKING

Depending on the type of grill that you are using, you can get the option to go for a Hot Smoking Method or a Cold Smoking One. However, the primary fact about these three different cooking techniques which you should keep in mind are as follows:

- **HOT SMOKING:** In this technique, the food will use both the heat on your grill and the smoke to prepare your food. This method is most suitable for chicken, lamb, brisket, etc.
- **COLD SMOKING:** In this method, you are going to smoke your meat at a very low temperature, such as 85 F (30 degrees Celsius), making sure that it doesn't come into direct contact with the heat. Cold smoking is mainly used
- **ROASTING SMOKE:** This is also known as Smoke Baking. This process is essentially a combined form of roasting and baking and can be performed in any smoker with a capacity to reach temperatures above 180 F (80 degrees Celsius).

SELECTING A SMOKER

You need to invest in a good smoker if you smoke meat regularly. Consider these options when buying a smoker. Here are two natural fire options for you:

CHARCOAL SMOKERS:

Are fueled by a combination of charcoal and wood. Charcoal burns quickly, and the temperature remains steady so you won't have any problem with a charcoal smoker. The wood gives a great flavor to the meat, and you will enjoy smoking meat.

WOOD SMOKER:

The wood smoker will give your brisket and ribs the best smoky flavor and taste, but it is harder to cook with wood. Both hardwood blocks and chips are used as fuel.

DIFFERENT SMOKER TYPES

You should know that in the market, you will get three different types of Smokers

CHARCOAL SMOKER:

These smokers are hands down the best for infusing the perfect smoky flavor to your meat. But be warned that these smokers are difficul2t to master as the method of regulating temperature is a little bit difficult compared to standard Gas or Electric smokers.

ELECTRIC SMOKER

After the charcoal smoker, next comes the more straightforward option, Electric Smokers. These are easy-to-use and plug-and-play types. All you need to do is plug in, set the temperature, and go about your daily life. The smoker will do the rest. However, remember that the smoky finishing flavor won't be as intense as the Charcoal one.

GAS SMOKERS

Finally, comes the Gas Smokers. These have a reasonably easy temperature control mechanism and are usually powered by LP Gas. The drawback of these Smokers is that you will have to keep checking up on your smoker now and then to ensure that it has enough Gas.

DIFFERENT SMOKER STYLES

The different styles of Smokers are essentially divided into the following.

VERTICAL (BULLET STYLE USING CHARCOAL)

These are usually low-cost solutions and are perfect for first-time smokers.

VERTICAL (CABINET STYLE)

These Smokers have a square-shaped design with cabinets and drawers/trays for easy accessibility. These cookers come with a water tray and a designated wood chips box.

OFFSET

These types of smokers have dedicated fireboxes that are attached to the side of the main grill. The smoke and heat required for these are generated from the firebox, which is passed through the main chamber and out through a nicely placed chimney.

KAMADO JOE

And finally, we have the Kamado Joe, which ceramic smokers are largely regarded as being the "Jack of All Trades."

These smokers can be used as low and slow smokers, grills, high or low-temperature ovens, and so on.

They have a thick ceramic wall that allows them to hold heat better than any other smoker, requiring only a little charcoal.

These are easy to use with better insulation and are more efficient when it comes to fuel control.

CHOOSE YOUR WOOD

You need to choose your wood carefully because the type of wood you will use affect significantly to the flavor and taste of the meat. Here are a few options for you:

- **MAPLE**: Maple has a smoky and sweet taste and goes well with pork or poultry
- **ALDER**: Alder is sweet and light. Perfect for poultry and fish.
- **APPLE**: Apple has a mild and sweet flavor. Goes well with pork, fish, and poultry.
- **OAK**: Oak is great for slow cooking. Ideal for game, pork, beef, and lamb.
- **MESQUITE**: Mesquite has a smoky flavor and is extremely strong. Goes well with pork or beef.
- **HICKORY**: Has a smoky and strong flavor. Goes well with beef and lamb.
- **CHERRY**: Has a mild and sweet flavor. Great for pork, beef, and turkey

THE DIFFERENT TYPES OF WOOD	SUITABLE FOR
HICKORY	WILD GAME, CHICKEN, PORK, CHEESES, BEEF
PECAN	CHICKEN, PORK, LAMB, CHEESES, FISH.
MESQUITE	BEEF AND VEGETABLES
ALDER	SWORDFISH, SALMON, STURGEON AND OTHER TYPES OF FISHES. WORKS WELL WITH PORK AND CHICKEN TOO.
OAK	BEEF OR BRISKETS
MAPLE	VEGETABLE, HAM OR POULTRY
CHERRY	GAME BIRDS, POULTRY OR PORK
APPLE	GAME BIRDS, POULTRY, BEEF
PEACH	GAME BIRDS, POULTRY OR PORK
GRAPE VINES	BEEF, CHICKEN OR TURKEY
WINE BARREL CHIPS	TURKEY, BEEF, CHICKEN OR CHEESES
SEAWEED	LOBSTER, MUSSELS, CRAB, SHRIMP ETC.
HERBS OR SPICES SUCH AS ROSEMARY, BAY LEAVES, MINT, LEMON PEELS, WHOLE NUTMEG ETC.	GOOD FOR CHEESES OR VEGETABLES AND A SMALL COLLECTION OF LIGHT MEATS SUCH AS FILLETS OR FISH STEAKS.

CHARCOAL

In General, there are three different types of charcoal. All of them are porous residues of black color made of carbon and ashes. However, the following are a little distinguishable due to their specific features.

- **BBQ BRIQUETTES:** These are the ones that are made from a fine blend of charcoal and char.

- **CHARCOAL BRIQUETTES:** These are created by compressing charcoal and are made from sawdust or wood products.

- **LUMP CHARCOAL:** These are made directly from hardwood and are the most premium quality charcoals. They are entirely natural and are free from any form of additives.

RIGHT TEMPERATURE

- Start at 250F (120C): Start your smoker a bit hot. This extra heat gets the smoking process going.

- Temperature drop: Once you add the meat to the smoker, the temperature will drop, which is fine.

- Maintain the temperature. Monitor and maintain the temperature. Keep the temperature steady during the smoking process.

Avoid peeking now and then. Smoke and heat are the two crucial elements that make your meat taste great. If you open the cover every now, and then you lose both of them, and your meat loses flavor. Only open the lid only when you truly need it.

BASIC PREPARATIONS

- Always be prepared to spend the whole day and take as much time as possible to smoke your meat for maximum effect.
- Ensure you obtain the perfect Ribs/Meat for the meal you are trying to smoke. Do a little bit of research if you need.
- I have already added a list of woods. Consult that list and choose the perfect wood for your meal.
- Make sure to prepare the marinade for each of the meals properly. A great deal of the flavors comes from the rubbing.
- Keep a meat thermometer handy to get the internal temperature when needed.
- Use mittens or tongs to keep yourself safe.
- Please refrain from using charcoal infused alongside starter fluid, as it might bring a very unpleasant odor to your food.
- Always start with a small amount of wood and keep adding them as you cook.
- Don't be afraid to experiment with different types of wood for newer flavors and experiences.
- Always keep a notebook near you and note jot down whatever you are doing or learning and use them during future sessions. A notebook will help you to evolve and move forward.

ELEMENTS OF SMOKING

Smoking is a very indirect method of cooking that relies on many factors to give you the most perfectly cooked meal you are looking for. Each component is essential to the whole process as they all work together to create the meal of your dreams.

- **TIME:** Unlike grilling or even Barbequing, smoking takes a long time and requires a lot of patience. It takes time for the smoky flavor to get infused into the meats slowly. Just to compare things, it takes about 8 minutes to thoroughly cook a steak through direct heating, while smoking (indirect heating) will take around 35-40 minutes.

- **TEMPERATURE:** When it comes to smoking, the temperature is affected by many factors that are not only limited to the wind and cold air temperatures but also the cooking wood's dryness. Some smokers work best with large fires that are controlled by the draw of a chimney and restricted airflow through the various vents of the cooking chamber and firebox. At the same time, other smokers tend to require minor fire with fewer coals and a completely different combination of the vent and draw controls. However, most smokers are designed to work at temperatures as low as 180 degrees Fahrenheit to as high as 300 degrees Fahrenheit. But the recommended temperature usually falls between 250 degrees Fahrenheit and 275 degrees Fahrenheit.

- **AIRFLOW:** The air to which the fire is significantly exposed determines how your fire will burn and how quickly it will burn the fuel. For instance, if you restrict airflow into the firebox by closing up the available vents, the fire will burn at a low temperature and vice versa. Typically in smokers, after lighting up the fire, the vents are opened to allow for maximum airflow and are then adjusted throughout the cooking process to ensure that optimum flame is achieved.

- **INSULATION:** Insulation is also essential for smokers as it helps to manage the cooking process throughout the whole cooking session. Good insulation allows smokers to reach the desired temperature instead of waiting hours!

SMOKING POINTS OF COOKING FATS & OILS

FAT/OIL	SMOKE POINT °F	SMOKE POINT °C
Safflower Oil	505-510°F	260-265°C
Rice Bran Oil	485-490°F	250-255°C
Light/Refined Olive Oil	460-465°F	235-240°C
Soybean Oil	445-450°F	230-235°C
Peanut Oil	445-450°F	230-235°C
Clarified Butter	445-450°F	230-235°C
Corn Oil	445-450°F	230-235°C
Sunflower Oil	435-440°F	220-225°C
Vegetable Oil	400-450°F	205-235°C
Beef Tallow	395-400°F	200-205°C
Canola Oil	395-400°F	200-205°C
Grapeseed Oil	385-390°F	195-200°C
Lard	365-370°F	185-190°C
Avocado Oil (Virgin)	370-400°F	190-205°C
Chicken Fat	370-375°F	190-195°C
Duck Fat	370-375°F	190-195°C
Vegetable Shortening	360-365°F	180-185°C
Sesame Oil	355-410°F	175-210°C
Butter	345-350°F	170-175°C
Coconut Oil	345-350°F	170-175°C
Extra-Virgin Olive Oil	320-370°F	160-190°C

CHAPTER 12 CAMPING
CAMPING WITH CAST IRON POTS

There are a lot of benefits to using a dutch oven and a skillet, and the most important are listed below:

1. The dutch oven and the skillet are flexible and can be used for different cooking methods on various heat sources. It gives you the versatility of bringing any heating elements and ingredients you prefer.
2. The dutch oven can be used for frying, boiling, stewing, baking, and roasting. It pretty much fills the need for every pan and pot you have.
3. The closing lid of the dutch oven doesn't let the hot air get out, and you can cook in the pot by filling in the ingredients and leaving it for several hours.
4. It brings up the flavor of your dish and makes it taste like a campfire while not making the ingredients burnt or extra bitter.
5. On a camping trip, if you accidentally bump into and hit the dutch oven with your tools and haphazardness, it can endure all the stress because of its incredible durability. There is no need to be too careful around this piece of device.

CHOOSING A DUTCH OVEN FOR CAMPING

You might buy a new dutch oven and be confused with all the options. You don't know what conditions should be met by the dutch oven for you to experience a hassle-free campfire dinner. Here is a list of criteria that you should look for when getting a dutch oven for camping, even second-hand.

1. It should at least have three legs for proper support and placement of the hot coals.
2. It should have a sturdy handle
3. The lid should close perfectly on the pot with little effort.
4. The thickness of the pot should be consistent all the way.
5. The thin handle attached to the pot is not weak and is easily movable.

It would be best to consider whether you have to feed a horde of people or need to provide two. There are five different sizes in which Dutch ovens are available, the smallest for two and the largest for feeding twenty people. The bigger the pot, the heavier it will be.

DUTCH OVEN USEFUL TIPS
THESE TOOLS ARE ESSENTIAL FOR SAFE AND PROPER COOKING ON A CAMPSITE.

- DUTCH OVEN OR A SKILLET
- COALS AND BRIQUETTES (NO. OF BAGS DEPENDS ON THE PERIOD OF THE TRIP)
- LONG TONGS WHICH WILL PLACE THE COALS
- LID LIFTER, SO YOU DON'T SCORCH YOURSELF.
- GLOVES THAT ARE HEAT RESISTANT
- SMALL BROOM OR BRUSH

HERE ARE THE STEPS NEEDED TO USE THE CAST IRON POT CORRECTLY:

START A CHARCOAL FIRE: USE A FIRE PIT OR A BARBECUE GRILL TO PLACE THE POT OVER THE BURNING COALS OR BRIQUETTES. YOU CAN ALSO PUT HOT COALS BENEATH THE POT ON A FLAT SURFACE.

PLACE YOUR INGREDIENTS: AFTER THE COALS START DOING THEIR THING, YOU CAN PUT YOUR INGREDIENTS IN THE POT AND CLOSE IT WITH THE LID.

ARRANGE THE COALS: IT WOULD HELP IF YOU PLACED THE COALS ABOVE AND BENEATH THE POT FOR EVEN AND HIGH-TEMPERATURE COOKING. YOU NEED TO PLACE THE COALS ACCORDING TO THE SIZE OF THE POT. IF YOUR POT SIZE IS 12 INCHES, YOU NEED TO PUT 12 COALS + 3 ON TOP AND 12 COALS -3 ON THE BOTTOM. IT WILL RAISE THE TEMPERATURE TO 350 F.

COVER THE FOOD AND WAIT: DON'T OPEN THE LID AGAIN AND AGAIN TO CHECK THE FOOD. IT CAN CAUSE THE ASHES AT THE TOP TO FALL INTO YOUR POT AND RUIN YOUR ENTIRE DISH. IF IT IS NECESSARY TO CHECK THE FOOD, THEN CAREFULLY USE THE LID LIFTER TO OPEN THE POT.

TAKE THE FOOD OUT WHEN DONE: BEFORE TAKING THE FOOD OUT, YOU HAVE TO REMOVE ALL THE ASHES FROM THE LID SO THE ASHES WILL NOT FALL INTO THE POT. FIRST, USE TONGS TO REMOVE THE COALS AND A BROOM TO REMOVE THE ASHES. NOW, USE A LID LIFTER TO OPEN THE LID. WEAR HEAT-RESISTANT GLOVES TO TOUCH THE POT AND SERVE YOUR MEAL.

THINGS YOU SHOULD AVOID WHEN USING A CAST IRON POT

- DON'T USE PLASTIC OR SILICONE UTENSILS
- DON'T PUT COLD WATER INTO A HOT POT. IT CAN CAUSE IT TO CRACK.
- DON'T DROP THE POT
- DON'T WASH IT WITH WIRE WOOL FOR ANY HARSH DETERGENT.
- DON'T LEAVE WATER IN IT. IT WILL CAUSE IT TO RUST.

THINGS YOU SHOULD FOLLOW WHEN USING A CAST IRON POT

- USE WOODEN UTENSILS
- PLACE THE DUTCH OVEN ON HEAT RESISTANT SURFACE
- TIGHTLY SECURE THE LID BEFORE USING THE DUTCH OVEN
- USE A SPONGE AND SOAP TO WASH THE POT
- SEASON YOUR POT AFTER EVERY USE.

CLEANING THE POTS

After you have made your meal, cleaning the pot is essential, so it remains in use for a long time.

1. Firstly, you put water into the pot until all the bits and scraps are submerged.
2. Now, heat the pot till the water starts to boil.
3. Add a few spoonfuls of baking soda and let the water bubble for a few minutes.
4. Use a wooden utensil to scrape off the bits.
5. When it looks clean, primarily, drain the water and scrub it with an abrasive sponge and soap.

CHAPTER 13 FOOD SAFETY
CLEANLINESS OF THE MEAT

If you can follow the steps below, you will be able to ensure that your meat is safe from any bacterial or airborne contamination.

This first step is essential as no market-bought or freshly cut meat is entirely sterile. Following these would significantly minimize the risk of getting affected by diseases.

- Make sure to properly wash your hands before beginning to process your meat. Use fresh tap water and soap/hand sanitizer.
- Make sure to remove metal ornaments such as rings and watches from your wrist and hand before handling the meat.
- Thoroughly clean the cutting surface using sanitizing liquid to remove any grease or unwanted contaminants. If you want a homemade sanitizer, you can simply make a solution of 1 part chlorine bleach and ten parts water.
- The sanitizer mentioned above should also be used to soak your tools, such as knives and other equipment, to ensure that they are safe to use.
- Alternatively, commercial acid based/ no rinsed sanitizers such as Star San will also work.
- After each use, all knives and other equipment, such as meat grinders, slicers, extruders, etc., should be cleaned thoroughly using soap water. The knives should be taken care in particular by cleaning the place just on top of the handle as it might contain blood and pieces of meat.
- When cleaning the surface, you should use cloths or sponges.

A note of sponges/clothes: It is ideal that you keep your sponge or cleaning cloth clean as it might result in cross-contamination. These are ideal harboring places for foodborne pathogens. Just follow the simple steps to ensure that you are on the safe side:

- Make sure to clean your sponge daily. It is seen that the effectiveness of cleaning it increases if you microwave the dam sponge for 1 minute and disinfect it using a solution of 1/4 -1/2 teaspoon of concentrated bleach. This process will kill 99% of bacteria.
- Replace your sponge frequently, as using the same sponge every time (even with wash) will result in eventual bacterial growth.
- When not using the sponge, please keep it dry and wring it off of any loose food or debris.

KEEPING YOUR MEAT COLD

Mismanagement of temperature is one of the most common reasons for outbreaks of foodborne diseases. The study has shown that bacteria grow best at temperatures of 40 to 140 degree Fahrenheit/4-60 degree Celsius, which means that if not taken care of properly, bacteria in the meat will start to multiply very quickly. The best way to prevent this is to keep your meat cold before using it. Keep them eat in your fridge before processing them and make sure that the temperature is below 40 degrees Fahrenheit/4 degree Celsius.

KEEPING YOUR MEAT COVERED

All foods start to diminish once they are opened from their packaging or exposed to the air. However, the effect can be greatly minimized if you cover or wrap the foods properly. The same goes for meat.

Good ways of keeping your meat covered and wrapped include:

- Using aluminum foil to cover up your meat will help to protect it from light and oxygen and keep the moisture intact. However, since Aluminum is reactive, it is advised that a layer of plastic wrap is used underneath the aluminum foil to provide a double protective coating.
- If the meat is kept in a bowl with no lid, then plastic wrap can seal the bowl, providing an airtight enclosure.
- Re-sealable bags protect by storing them in a bag and squeezing out any air.
- Airtight glass or plastic containers with lids are good options as well.
- A type of paper known as Freezer paper is specifically designed to wrap foods to be kept in the fridge. These wraps are excellent for meat as well.

Vacuum sealers are often used for Sous Vide packaging. These machines are a bit expensive but can provide excellent packaging by completely sucking out any air from a re-sealable bag. This greatly increases the meat's shelf life outside and in the fridge.

PREVENTING FORMS OF CROSS-CONTAMINATION

Cross-Contamination usually occurs when one food comes into contact with another. In our case, we are talking about our meats.

This can be avoided very easily by keeping the following things in check:

- Always wash your hands thoroughly with warm water. The cutting boards, counters, knives, and other utensils should also be cleaned as instructed in the chapter's first section.
- Keep different types of meat in separate bowls, dishes, and plates before using them.
- When storing the meat in the fridge, keep the raw meat, seafood, poultry, and eggs on the bottom shelf of your fridge and in individual sealed containers.
- Keep your refrigerator shelves cleaned, and juices from meat/vegetables might drip on them.
- Always refrain from keeping raw meat/vegetables on the same plate as cooked goods.
- Always clean your cutting boards and use different cutting boards for different foods. Raw meats, vegetables, and other foods should be cut using a different table.

KNIVES

KNIVES: Sharp knives should be used to slice the meat accordingly. While using the knife, you should keep the following in mind.

- Always make sure to use a sharp knife
- Never hold a knife under your arm or leave it under a piece of meat
- Always keep your knives within visible distance
- Always keep your knife point down
- Always cut down towards the cutting surface and away from your body
- Never allow children to toy with knives unattended
- Wash the knives while cutting different types of food

RECIPES INDEX

CONCLUSION

I am happy to share this cookbook with you, and I take pride in offering you an extensive array of recipes that you will love and enjoy. I hope you benefit from each of our recipes, and I am sure you will like all the recipes we have offered you. Don't hesitate to try our creative and easy-to-make recipes, and remember that I have put my heart into coming up with delicious meals for you. If you like my recipes, you can share them with acquaintances and friends. I need your encouragement to continue writing more books!
P.S. Thank you for reading this book. If you've enjoyed this book, please don't shy; drop me a line, leave feedback, or both on Amazon. I love reading feedback and your opinion is extremely important to me.

Printed in Great Britain
by Amazon